Down Home

DIABETIC RECIPES

Braised Lamb with Be

Vanilla Pound Cake, page 59

DELICIOUS WAYS
TO CONTROL **DIABETES**

Down Home
DIABETIC RECIPES

Compiled and edited by
Anne C. Cain, M.S., M.P.H., R.D.

Oxmoor
House®

©2003 by Oxmoor House, Inc.
Book Division of Southern Progress Corporation
P.O. Box 2463, Birmingham, Alabama 35201

ISBN: 0-8487-2623-5
ISSN: 1523-8032
Printed in the United States of America
First Printing 2003

Be sure to check with your health-care provider
before making any changes in your diet.

Editor-in-Chief: Nancy Fitzpatrick Wyatt
Executive Editor: Katherine M. Eakin
Art Director: Cynthia R. Cooper
Copy Chief: Catherine Ritter Scholl

Delicious Ways to Control Diabetes
Down Home Diabetic Recipes

Editor: Anne Chappell Cain, M.S., M.P.H., R.D.
Assistant Editor: Heather Averett
Editorial Assistant: Diane Rose
Director, Test Kitchens: Elizabeth Tyler Luckett
Assistant Director, Test Kitchens: Julie Christopher
Recipe Editor: Gayle Hays Sadler
Test Kitchens Staff: Kristi Carter, Nicole Faber, Jan A. Smith,
    Elise Weis, Kelly Wilton
Senior Photographer: Jim Bathie
Photographer: Brit Huckabay
Senior Photo Stylist: Kay E. Clarke
Photo Stylist: Ashley J. Wyatt
Publishing Systems Administrator: Rick Tucker
Director, Production and Distribution: Phillip Lee
Books Production Manager: Greg Amason
Production Assistant: Faye Porter Bonner

Contributors:
Designer: Carol O. Loria
Copy Editor: Dolores Hydock
Indexer: Mary Ann Laurens
Photo Stylists: Melanie Clarke, Connie Formby
Medical Advisor: David DeAtkine, Jr., M.D.

To order additional publications, call 1-800-765-6400
or visit **oxmoorhouse.com**

Cover: Strawberry Shortcakes, page 56

CONTENTS

Dear Friends,

Food has the power to evoke vivid and pleasurable memories. Have you ever gotten a whiff of fresh-baked biscuits and experienced not only the taste of butter and jelly, but also felt the warmth and love in your grandmother's kitchen? Often, the mere mention of a specific food can take us back to a memorable time and place.

It's no wonder that when we think of family and special occasions, we think of food. And in times of uncertainty and anxiety, who among us does not yearn for the comforts of home and food? If you have diabetes and think you must give up many of the foods you love, I have some great news!

With *Down Home Diabetic Recipes,* you can enjoy your favorite foods, but in a new and healthier way. Our staff of registered dietitians and cooking experts has put together over 140 homestyle recipes with reduced sugar and fat, while keeping the same familiar down-home flavor that you long for. There's a whole chapter of casseroles alone, plus breads, soups, sandwiches, desserts, and a special holiday menu chapter. You'll also get a one-week menu planner that uses recipes from the book to assist you in meal preparation. Each recipe has nutrient information and exchanges, so you can easily work the food into your meal plan. You'll also find some friendly advice on controlling diabetes, plus a new "Well Preserved" feature showing you how to make low-sugar jams and jellies. *Down Home Diabetic Recipes* lets you enjoy the foods you remember from your past, but in a healthier way, assuring good times and good health for your future.

> # Food has a rare ability to carry you back... it can be counted on to produce a sensation in time present that will duplicate a sensation from time past.
>
> **MICHAEL FRANK,**
> *American editor and author*

Sincerely,

Anne Cain

Anne Cain, Editor

6

OVER THE FENCE

Like meeting a neighbor over the picket fence to chat about the latest news, "Over the Fence" brings you a friendly update on the latest in diabetes. We hope it makes your life with diabetes a little easier.

Have You Heard?

If you or someone in your family has diabetes, there's a lot to talk about.

Home Lab A new Hemoglobin A1C (HbA1C) home test kit can help you get an overall picture of your diabetes control. The HbA1C value indicates your average blood glucose for the past 2 to 3 months. Your doctor probably orders this test at your routine visits.

There are two types of kits: a one-time kit that gives results in 8 minutes, and a mail-in test where you mail in a blood sample to a lab. Both types of kits cost about $25.

At Your Fingertips Several of the new blood glucose monitoring devices use sites other than the fingertips. While it's nice to have a break from fingersticks, research shows that fingerstick tests generally detect low blood glucose earlier than tests performed with capillary blood from the arms or thighs. You should avoid using alternate sites when blood glucose is likely to be changing rapidly, such as after meals and right after an insulin injection. Talk to your diabetes educator about which type of meter is best for you.

Milking It Weight control is easier for people who get plenty of calcium in their diet. It appears that when calcium intake is low, your body tends to store more fat.

Tax Breaks for Weight The Internal Revenue Service (IRS) now allows medical deductions for weight-loss programs. If you have a condition such as type 2 diabetes in which you would benefit from losing weight, you're eligible for the tax break. You can't deduct health club memberships or special diet foods, but you can deduct the cost of doctor-recommended weight-loss programs, weight-loss surgery, services of dietitians, and weight-loss programs such as Weight Watchers®.

We've Got You Covered

Don't pay more for diabetes supplies and medications than you need to. Your insurance may cover more than you think.

The American Diabetes Association (ADA) has worked tirelessly to establish laws requiring state-regulated health plans to cover the cost of diabetes supplies and services. Currently, 46 states have put these laws into effect. Similar legislation is being introduced in the remaining states (Alabama, Idaho, North Dakota, and Ohio) with hopes it will be adopted by the end of 2003.

The ADA has also worked with Congress in regards to Medicare coverage. Medicare is now required by law to cover the costs of glucose monitoring supplies, insulin pumps, and diabetes education services. To see if you qualify for Medicare coverage, call the Medicare hotline at 1-800-638-6833.

For any other diabetes insurance coverage information, call the ADA at 1-800-DIABETES or visit their web site at www.diabetes.org.

Go Nuts!

If you quit eating peanut butter because you thought it was unhealthy, it may be time to welcome it back to the table. A recent study found that peanut butter may actually help fend off diabetes.

More than 83,000 women participated in the study, and those who ate a handful of nuts (or one tablespoon of peanut butter) at least five times a week were less likely to develop type 2 diabetes than the women who rarely or never ate nuts. It appears that the fiber and magnesium in nuts may help the body maintain balanced insulin and glucose levels.

Here are some ways to add peanuts and peanut butter to your diet. Our recipe for Homemade Peanut Butter on page 29 is a great place to start. Or try some of these nutty treats:

• **Spread** peanut butter on whole wheat toast for breakfast.

• **Melt** a small amount of peanut butter in the microwave and spoon over no-added-sugar ice cream.

• **Sprinkle** chopped nuts on a mixed green salad.

• **Stir** chopped peanuts into low-fat yogurt.

On the Road

When you travel with diabetes, by land, air, or sea, plan ahead and pack some common sense.

☐ Ask your physician for a letter explaining your condition and the medication and supplies you need. Ask for extra prescriptions in case your medications are lost.

☐ Take a list of your medical history, medications, drug allergies, and emergency numbers.

☐ Keep your medications and supplies in your carry-on bag instead of in checked luggage.

☐ Pack a low blood sugar emergency kit.

☐ Pack at least twice the amount of insulin and supplies you think you'll use.

☐ Pack plenty of snacks in case meal plans are interrupted.

☐ If you are changing time zones, ask a member of your health-care team how to adjust your insulin needs. If you wear a pump, remember to reset the pump's clock to your new time zone.

☐ Get a medical ID bracelet, necklace, or watch ID tag.

☐ Pack your insulin in an insulated travel pack—it does not have to be refrigerated—to ensure it doesn't get too hot or too cold. Don't store insulin in the trunk or glove compartment of a car or in the overhead bin of an airplane.

☐ Pack a hard plastic container to store used needles and lancets.

☐ Test your blood glucose often. Jet lag, which is marked by fatigue, irritability, and difficulty concentrating, mirrors low blood sugar.

☐ Call the airline to request diabetic or low-fat meals in advance.

Portable Snacks

Here are some ideas for snacks to pack for travel, including the carbohydrate and exchange values.

1 package crackers with spreadable cheese: 1 Starch, 1 Fat; 10g carb

1 package sandwich crackers with peanut butter or cheese: 2 Starch, 2 Fat; 23g carb

1 (1⅛-ounce) bag low-fat potato chips: 2 Starch; 26g carb

8 animal crackers: 1 Starch; 15g carb

6 saltine crackers: 1 Starch; 15g carb

6 three-ring pretzels: 1 Starch; 15g carb

1 fruit roll: 1 Starch or Fruit; 15g carb

1 granola bar: 1 Starch, 1 Fat; 15g carb

1 (1.3-ounce) bar toasted rice and marshmallow snack square: 2 Starch; 30g carb

1 mini box raisins (2 tablespoons): 1 Fruit; 11g carb

Abbreviations Key: g = grams; carb = carbohydrate

IN THE KITCHEN

There's no need to give up your favorite foods when you have diabetes. With a few simple substitutions, you can turn most any high-sugar, high-fat recipe into a healthy, family-pleasing dish.

Banana Pudding

1   (1.5-ounce) package vanilla sugar-free instant pudding mix
1   (1-ounce) package vanilla sugar-free instant pudding mix
5   cups fat-free milk
1   (8-ounce) container low-fat sour cream
1   (8-ounce) container frozen reduced-calorie whipped topping, thawed, divided
1   (5.5-ounce) package sugar-free vanilla wafers (about 45 wafers), divided
7   ripe bananas, sliced

Combine pudding mixes and prepare according to package directions, using 5 cups milk and a wire whisk. Add sour cream and one-third of whipped topping to pudding; stir well.
Line a 13 x 9-inch baking dish with vanilla wafers; reserve remaining wafers.
Arrange banana over wafers. Pour pudding mixture over bananas. Line edge of dish with wafers, reserving 4 wafers to crumble and sprinkle on top.
Cover and chill at least 3 hours.
Spread remaining whipped topping over pudding. Cover and chill. Sprinkle crumbled wafers over topping before serving. **Yield:** 15 servings (serving size: about 1 cup).

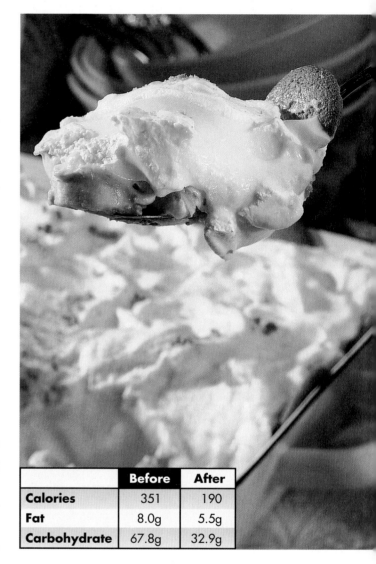

	Before	After
Calories	351	190
Fat	8.0g	5.5g
Carbohydrate	67.8g	32.9g

Per Serving: Calories 190   Protein 5.0g   Fat 5.5g   (sat 3.3g)   Carbohydrate 32.9g   Fiber 1.5g   Cholesterol 7mg   Sodium 89mg
Exchanges: 1 Starch, 1 Fruit, 1 Fat

HOW WE LIGHTENED IT

Banana Pudding might just be the ultimate comfort food. Here, we've made some changes to the traditional recipe, giving you a healthier version of a homestyle favorite.

Healthy Substitutions

- Instead of making a custard, simplify and use sugar-free instant pudding mix.

- You can omit the eggs, sugar, and flour when you use pudding mix instead of preparing a custard.

- Use fat-free milk instead of whole milk to prepare the pudding.

- Add low-fat sour cream to the pudding mixture to make it creamier without adding much fat.

- Use sugar-free vanilla wafers instead of original vanilla wafers.*

- Top pudding with frozen reduced-calorie whipped topping instead of a meringue.

*Note: Even though we've substituted sugar-free vanilla wafers, you can still use the regular ones. There's not much difference in carbohydrate values between the regular and the sugar-free wafers. One serving of regular wafers (8 wafers) has 21 grams of carbohydrate; one serving of sugar-free wafers (9 wafers) has 19 grams.

Banana Pudding

omit, use sugar-free instant pudding mix

3$^1/_2$ tablespoons all-purpose flour

1$^1/_3$ cups sugar

Dash of salt

3   large eggs, separated

3   cups milk *use fat-free milk*

1   teaspoon vanilla extract

use frozen reduced-calorie whipped topping

1   (12-ounce) package vanilla wafers *use sugar-free vanilla wafers*

6   medium bananas

$^1/_4$ cup plus 2 tablespoons sugar

1   teaspoon vanilla extract

Combine first 3 ingredients in a heavy saucepan. Beat egg yolks; combine egg yolks and milk, stirring well. Stir into dry ingredients; cook over medium heat, stirring constantly, until smooth and thickened. Remove from heat; stir in 1 teaspoon vanilla. Layer one-third of wafers in a 3-quart baking dish. Slice 2 bananas, and layer over wafers. Pour one-third of custard over bananas. Repeat layers twice.
Beat egg whites at high speed with an electric mixer until foamy. Gradually add $^1/_4$ cup plus 2 tablespoons sugar, 1 tablespoon at a time, beating until stiff peaks form. Add 1 teaspoon vanilla, and beat until blended.
Spread meringue over custard, sealing to edge of dish. Bake at 325° for 25 to 30 minutes or until golden. *Yield: 12 servings.*

LOW-FAT INGREDIENT SUBSTITUTIONS
Use these substitutions to "lighten up" any of your own favorite recipes.

Needed Ingredient	Substitutions
FATS AND OILS	
Butter or margarine	Reduced-calorie stick margarine or light stick butter in baked products; reduced-calorie margarine, light butter, or yogurt-based spread
Mayonnaise	Fat-free, reduced-fat, or low-fat mayonnaise
Oil	Safflower, soybean, corn, canola, or peanut oil in reduced amount
Salad dressing	Fat-free or oil-free dressing
Shortening	Soybean, corn, canola, or peanut oil in amount reduced by one-third
DAIRY PRODUCTS	
Cheeses: American, Cheddar, colby, Edam, or Swiss	Reduced-fat and part-skim cheeses with 5 grams of fat or less per ounce
Cheese, cottage	Fat-free or 1% low-fat cottage cheese
Cheese, cream	Fat-free, 1/3-less-fat, or tub-style light cream cheese
Cheese, ricotta	Fat-free, light, or part-skim ricotta cheese
Cream, sour	Low-fat or fat-free sour cream; low-fat or fat-free yogurt
Cream, whipping	Chilled fat-free evaporated milk or fat-free half-and-half
Ice cream	Fat-free or low-fat frozen yogurt; fat-free or low-fat ice cream; sherbet; sorbet
Milk, whole	Fat-free, low-fat, or reduced-fat milk
MEATS, FISH, POULTRY, AND EGGS	
Bacon	Canadian bacon; turkey bacon; lean ham
Beef, ground	Extra lean or ultralean ground beef; freshly ground raw turkey
Beef, lamb, pork, or veal	Chicken, turkey, or lean cuts of meat trimmed of all visible fat
Luncheon meat	Skinned, sliced turkey or chicken breast; lean ham; lean roast beef
Poultry	Skinned poultry
Tuna packed in oil	Tuna packed in water
Turkey, self-basting	Turkey basted with fat-free broth
Egg, whole	2 egg whites or 1/4 cup fat-free egg substitute
MISCELLANEOUS	
Fudge sauce	Fat-free fudge sauce or chocolate syrup
Nuts	Reduce amount one-third to one-half, and toast
Soups, canned	98%-fat-free or reduced-fat, reduced-sodium condensed cream soups

WELL PRESERVED

A Guide to Jams & Jellies

To make sugar-free jams and jellies, you can either use a pectin that's for low-sugar recipes or a recipe that calls for unflavored gelatin.

The Right Pectin

If you're using pectin, you must use a *low-methoxyl pectin* (no-sugar-needed pectin), a special kind of pectin that helps fruit gel without sugar. Look for Ball No-Sugar-Needed Fruit Jell Pectin, Slimset, Mrs. Wages, Jamit, or Walnut Acres. The product should have a statement on the label that says the product is "for making homemade jams and jellies with low or no sugar."

Since this type of pectin does not need sugar to form a gel, the sweetness will come from the fruit, fruit juice, and/or sugar substitute.

Sugar aids in gel formation, so jams and jellies made without sugar tend to have a soft set. Refrigerate if you want a firmer spread.

Canning Procedures

Follow the manufacturer's directions for processing that are enclosed in the package of pectin. *Don't use old recipes or procedures from old cookbooks; canning methods have changed over the years and the old methods may not be safe.* If properly processed and sealed, sugar-free jams and jellies can be stored in a cool, dry, dark area up to one year. Or store them in the refrigerator.

These jams and jellies were processed using standard lids and bands. The bands were replaced with screw-on lids for decorative use.

Try some of these "pick-of-the-season" jams and jellies and taste the goodness of summer in a jar.

Strawberry Jam

8 cups fresh strawberries
1½ cups unsweetened apple juice, divided
¾ cup Sugar Twin
1 tablespoon lemon juice
2 envelopes unflavored gelatin

Wash and hull strawberries. Process in a food processor until chopped. Place berries, 1 cup apple juice, sugar substitute, and lemon juice in a Dutch oven. Bring to a boil over medium-high heat; reduce heat, and simmer, uncovered, 20 minutes or until slightly thick, stirring often.

Sprinkle gelatin over remaining ½ cup juice; let stand 5 minutes. Stir gelatin mixture into berry mixture; cook 1 to 2 minutes or until gelatin dissolves.

Pour into hot sterilized jars, leaving ¼ inch at the top of jar; wipe jar rims. Cover at once with metal lids, and screw on bands. Process in boiling water bath 5 minutes. **Yield:** 4 cups.

Per Tablespoon: Calories 8   Protein 0.3g
Fat 0.1g   (sat 0.0g)   Carbohydrate 1.6g   Fiber 0.3g
Cholesterol 0mg   Sodium 1mg
Exchange: Free (up to 3 tablespoons)

Raspberry Jam

Use 8 cups fresh raspberries for strawberries, and add 2 tablespoons granulated sugar to berry mixture.

Combine berry mixture, 1 cup apple juice, ¾ cup sugar substitute, and 1 tablespoon lemon juice in a Dutch oven. Bring to a boil over medium-high heat; reduce heat, and simmer, uncovered, 20 minutes or until slightly thick, stirring often. Strain mixture, and discard seeds. Sprinkle 2 envelopes gelatin over ½ cup apple juice, and proceed as directed for Strawberry Jam. **Yield:** 4 cups.

Per Tablespoon: Calories 13   Protein 0.3g
Fat 0.1g   (sat 0.0g)   Carbohydrate 2.9g   Fiber 1.1g
Cholesterol 0mg   Sodium 1mg
Exchange: Free (up to 2 tablespoons)

Peach-Orange Jam

12 cups sliced fresh peaches
1 (1¾-ounce) package no-sugar-needed pectin
1¾ cups Equal Spoonful
2 (0.3-ounce) tubs orange sugar-free drink mix (such as Crystal Light)

Process peaches in a food processor until chopped. Transfer peaches to a Dutch oven; stir in pectin. Let stand 10 minutes. Bring to a boil over medium-high heat; cook 15 minutes, stirring constantly. Remove from heat.

Safety Tips for Jams and Jellies

1. Wash and rinse jars, and examine for nicks and cracks.

2. Sterilize jars in a boiling water bath at least 10 minutes. Keep jars warm in dishwasher or in hot water until ready to fill.

3. Wash and rinse lids and bands. Place lids in a small saucepan of water. Bring to a simmer; remove from heat (do not boil). Keep lids in warm water until ready to use.

4. Check lids for seal by pressing down on the center of lid. If lid springs up, it hasn't sealed, and these jars must be stored in the refrigerator.

Stir in sugar substitute and drink mix. Pour into hot sterilized jars, leaving ¼ inch at the top of jar; wipe jar rims. Cover at once with metal lids, and screw on bands. Process in boiling water bath 5 minutes. **Yield:** 8 cups.

Per Tablespoon: Calories 9   Protein 0.1g
Fat 0.0g   (sat 0.0g)   Carbohydrate 2.4g   Fiber 0.4g
Cholesterol 0mg   Sodium 0mg
Exchange: Free (up to 2 tablespoons)

Grape Jelly

2 (11.5-ounce) cans no-sugar-added frozen
    concentrated grape juice, thawed (such as
    Welch's 100% Grape Juice)

1½ cups water

1   (1¾-ounce) package no-sugar-needed pectin

¾   cup Equal Spoonful

Combine grape juice concentrate and water in a 2-quart glass measuring cup. Gradually add pectin, stirring well. Let mixture stand 5 minutes. Microwave at HIGH until mixture comes to a rolling boil, stirring after 4 minutes. Boil 1 minute. Remove from heat; skim foam if necessary. Add sugar substitute, stirring until sugar substitute is completely dissolved.

Pour mixture into hot sterilized jars, leaving ¼ inch at the top of jar; wipe jar rims. Cover at once with metal lids, and screw on bands. Process in boiling water bath 5 minutes. **Yield:** 4⅓ cups.

Per Tablespoon: Calories 31   Protein 0.0g
Fat 0.0g   (sat 0.0g)   Carbohydrate 8.0g   Fiber 0.2g
Cholesterol 0mg   Sodium 0mg
Exchange: ½ Fruit

MENU PLANNER

A Week of Homestyle Meals

DOWN-HOME RECIPES

The recipes in bold are recipes from this cookbook, and the page numbers are provided for easy reference. The other items, such as fresh fruits, vegetables, breads, and grains, are simple ways to round out the meals. If you want to substitute another recipe from the book in a particular menu, choose one with similar calorie, carbohydrate, and exchange values.

CALORIE LEVELS

For each day, we've given you three different calorie levels: 1500, 1800, and 2000. The daily calorie percentage is approximately 55 percent calories from carbohydrate, 20 percent from protein, and 25 percent or less from fat. The exchange values for each meal are listed below the menu. Use your own meal plan to determine the specific number of servings you can have or the number of other items you can add.

PERSONAL MEAL PLANS

Use these menus and the recipes in the book to make your meal plan work for you. Since meal and snack plans differ according to dietary treatments and goals, this weekly menu planner is simply a guide to recipes and food items that make pleasing meals.

MONDAY

	1500 calories	1800 calories	2000 calories
BREAKFAST	Whole wheat bagel, 1 small Light cream cheese, 2 tbsp Mixed berries, ¾ c Fat-free milk, 1 c 2 Starch, 1 Fruit, 1 Meat, 1 Milk, 1 Fat	Whole wheat bagel, 1½ small Light cream cheese, 4 tbsp Mixed berries, ¾ c Fat-free milk, 1 c 3 Starch, 1 Fruit, 1 Meat, 1 Milk, 2 Fat	Whole wheat bagel, 1½ small Light cream cheese, 4 tbsp Mixed berries, ¾ c Fat-free milk, 1 c 3 Starch, 1 Fruit, 1 Meat, 1 Milk, 2 Fat
LUNCH	**Canadian BLT,** *page 158,* 1 serving **Caraway Coleslaw,** *page 114,* 1 serving Melon balls, 1 c 2 Starch, 2 Veg, 1 Fruit, 1½ Meat, 1 Fat	**Canadian BLT,** *page 158,* 1 serving **Caraway Coleslaw,** *page 114,* 1 serving Melon balls, 1 c No-sugar-added, fat-free ice cream, 1 c 3 Starch, 2 Veg, 1 Fruit, 1½ Meat, 1 Fat	**Canadian BLT,** *page 158,* 1 serving **Caraway Coleslaw,** *page 114,* 1 serving Melon balls, 1 c No-sugar-added, fat-free ice cream, 1 c 3 Starch, 2 Veg, 1 Fruit, 1½ Meat, 1 Fat
DINNER	**Easy Barbecued Chicken,** *page 96,* 1 serving **Hearty Mashed Potatoes,** *page 138,* 1 serving Green peas, ⅓ c Orange sections, ¾ cup Light butter, 1 tbsp 2½ Starch, 1½ Veg, 1 Fruit, 4 Meat, 1½ Fat	**Easy Barbecued Chicken,** *page 96,* 1 serving **Hearty Mashed Potatoes,** *page 138,* 1 serving Green peas, ⅓ c Orange sections, ¾ cup Light butter, 1 tbsp 2½ Starch, 1½ Veg, 1 Fruit, 4 Meat, 1½ Fat	**Easy Barbecued Chicken,** *page 96,* 1 serving **Hearty Mashed Potatoes,** *page 138,* 2 servings Green peas, ⅔ c Orange sections, ¾ cup Light butter, 1 tbsp Fat-free milk, 1 c 4 Starch, 3 Veg, 1 Fruit, 4 Meat, 2 Fat
SNACK	Turkey sandwich (1 oz turkey, 1 slice whole wheat bread) Fat-free milk, ½ c 1 Starch, 1 Meat, ½ Milk	Turkey sandwich (1 oz turkey, 1 slice whole wheat bread, 1 tbsp mayonnaise) Fat-free milk, 1 c 1 Starch, 1 Meat 1 Milk, 1 Fat	Turkey sandwich (1 oz turkey, 1 slice whole wheat bread, 1 tbsp mayonnaise) Fat-free milk, 1 c 1 Starch, 1 Meat, 1 Milk, 1 Fat

Abbreviations Key: **tbsp** = tablespoon(s)   **tsp** = teaspoon(s)   **oz** = ounce(s)   **c** = cup(s)

TUESDAY

1500 calories	1800 calories	2000 calories
Blueberry Muffins, *page 38,* 2 muffins Light butter, 2 tbsp Fat-free milk, 1 c	**Blueberry Muffins,** *page 38,* 2 muffins Light butter, 2 tbsp Fat-free milk, 1 c	**Blueberry Muffins,** *page 38,* 2 muffins Light butter, 1 tbsp Bacon, 2 slices Fat-free milk, 1 c
2 Starch, 2 Fruit, 1 Milk, 2 Fat	2 Starch, 2 Fruit, 1 Milk, 2 Fat	2 Starch, 2 Fruit, 1 Meat, 1 Milk, 3 Fat
Crab Cakes, *page 72,* 1 serving Corn on the cob, 1 ear Cucumber and tomato salad, 1 c Reduced-fat Italian dressing, 2 tbsp Apple, 1	**Crab Cakes,** *page 72,* 1 serving Corn on the cob, 2 ears Light butter, 1 tbsp Cucumber and tomato salad, 1 c Reduced-fat Italian dressing, 2 tbsp Apple, 1	**Crab Cakes,** *page 72,* 1 serving Corn on the cob, 2 ears Light butter, 2 tbsp Cucumber and tomato salad, 1 c Reduced-fat Italian dressing, 2 tbsp Apple, 1
2 Starch, 1 Veg, 1 Fruit, 3½ Meat, 2 Fat	3 Starch, 1 Veg, 1 Fruit, 3½ Meat, 2 Fat	3 Starch, 1 Veg, 1 Fruit, 3½ Meat, 3 Fat
Apricot-Glazed Ham Steak, *page 90,* 1 serving **Turnip Greens with Canadian Bacon,** *page 136,* 1 serving Baked sweet potato, 1 small Light butter, 1 tbsp Whole wheat roll, 1	**Apricot-Glazed Ham Steak,** *page 90,* 1 serving **Turnip Greens with Canadian Bacon,** *page 136,* 1 serving Baked sweet potato, 1 small Light butter, 2 tbsp Whole wheat roll, 2	**Apricot-Glazed Ham Steak,** *page 90,* 1 serving **Turnip Greens with Canadian Bacon,** *page 136,* 1 serving Baked sweet potato, 1 small Light butter, 2 tbsp Whole wheat roll, 2
2 Starch, 1½ Veg, ½ Fruit, 2½ Meat, 1 Fat	3 Starch, 1½ Veg, ½ Fruit, 2½ Meat, 2 Fat	3 Starch, 1½ Veg, ½ Fruit, 2½ Meat, 2 Fat
Homemade Peanut Butter, *page 29,* 2 tbsp Graham crackers, 3 (2½-inch) squares	**Homemade Peanut Butter,** *page 29,* 2 tbsp Graham crackers, 3 (2½-inch) squares	**Homemade Peanut Butter,** *page 29,* 2 tbsp Graham crackers, 6 (2½-inch) squares
1 Starch, 1 Meat, 1½ Fat	1 Starch, 1 Meat, 1½ Fat	2 Starch, 1 Meat, 1½ Fat

WEDNESDAY

1500 calories	1800 calories	2000 calories
Cheese toast (2 slices whole wheat toast, 2 slices low-fat cheese) Cantaloupe, ⅓ Fat-free milk, ½ c	Cheese toast (2 slices whole wheat toast, 2 slices low-fat cheese) Cantaloupe, ⅓ Fat-free milk, 1 c	Cheese toast (2 slices whole wheat toast, 2 slices low-fat cheese) Cantaloupe, ⅓ Whole grain cereal, ½ c Fat-free milk, 1 c
2 Starch, 1 Fruit, 2 Meat, ½ Milk	2 Starch, 1 Fruit, 2 Meat, 1 Milk, 1 Fat	2 Starch, 1 Fruit, 2 Meat, 1 Milk, 1 Fat
Smoked Chicken Club Sandwich, *page 161,* 1 serving Carrot sticks, ½ c **Summertime Lemonade,** *page 22,* 1 serving	**Smoked Chicken Club Sandwich,** *page 161,* 1 serving Carrot sticks, ½ c **Summertime Lemonade,** *page 22,* 1 serving	**Smoked Chicken Club Sandwich,** *page 161,* 1 serving Carrot sticks, 1 c **Summertime Lemonade,** *page 22,* 1 serving
3 Starch, 1 Veg, ½ Fruit, 2 Meat, 1 Fat	3 Starch, 1 Veg, ½ Fruit, 2 Meat, 1 Fat	3 Starch, 2 Veg, ½ Fruit, 2 Meat, 1 Fat
Beef Stroganoff, *page 83,* 1 serving Steamed broccoli, ½ c Fresh blackberries, ¾ c	**Beef Stroganoff,** *page 83,* 1 serving Steamed broccoli, 1 c Light butter, 1 tbsp **Blackberry Cobbler,** *page 63,* 1 serving	**Beef Stroganoff,** *page 83,* 1 serving Steamed broccoli, 1 c Light butter, 1 tbsp **Blackberry Cobbler,** *page 63,* 1 serving
3 Starch, 1 Veg, 1 Fruit, 4 Meat, 1 Fat	4 Starch, 2 Veg, 1½ Fruit, 4 Meat, 1 Fat	4 Starch, 2 Veg, 1½ Fruit, 4 Meat, 1 Fat
Wheat crackers, 5 Cheddar cheese, 1 oz	Wheat crackers, 5 Cheddar cheese, 1 oz	Wheat crackers, 10 Cheddar cheese, 2 oz
1 Starch, 1 Meat, 1 Fat	1 Starch, 1 Meat, 1 Fat	2 Starch, 2 Meat, 2 Fat

THURSDAY

	1500 calories	1800 calories	2000 calories
BREAKFAST	**Cinnamon Rolls,** *page 46,* 2 rolls Fresh blueberries, ¾ c Fat-free milk, ½ c	**Cinnamon Rolls,** *page 46,* 2 rolls Fresh blueberries, ¾ c Fat-free milk, 1 c	**Cinnamon Rolls,** *page 46,* 2 rolls Fresh blueberries, ¾ c Fat-free milk, 1 c
	3 Starch, 1 Fruit, ½ Milk, 1 Fat	3 Starch, 1 Fruit, 1 Milk, 1 Fat	3 Starch, 1 Fruit, 1 Milk, 1 Fat
LUNCH	**Macaroni and Cheese Soup,** *page 147,* 1 serving Saltine crackers, 6 Apple, 1	**Macaroni and Cheese Soup,** *page 147,* 1 serving Saltine crackers, 6 Apple, 1 Fat-free milk, 1 c	**Macaroni and Cheese Soup,** *page 147,* 1 serving Saltine crackers, 12 Apple, 1 Fat-free milk, 1 c
	2 Starch, 2 Veg, 1 Fruit, 1 Meat, 1 Fat	2 Starch, 2 Veg, 1 Fruit, 1 Milk, 1 Meat, 1 Fat	3 Starch, 2 Veg, 1 Fruit, 1 Milk, 1 Meat, 1 Fat
DINNER	**Shrimp Scampi,** *page 76,* 1 serving Green beans, 1 c Red grapes, 1 c	**Shrimp Scampi,** *page 76,* 1 serving Green beans, 1 c French bread drizzled with 1 tsp olive oil, 1 slice Red grapes, 1 c	**Shrimp Scampi,** *page 76,* 1 serving Green beans, 1 c French bread drizzled with 2 tsp olive oil, 2 slices Red grapes, 1 c
	2 Starch, 2 Veg, 1 Fruit, 4 Meat,	3 Starch, 2 Veg, 1 Fruit, 4 Meat, 1 Fat	4 Starch, 2 Veg, 1 Fruit, 4 Meat, 2 Fat
SNACK	**Oatmeal-Raisin Cookies,** *page 55,* 2 cookies Fat-free milk, 1 c	**Oatmeal-Raisin Cookies,** *page 55,* 2 cookies Fat-free milk, 1 c	**Oatmeal-Raisin Cookies,** *page 55,* 3 cookies Fat-free milk, 1 c
	2 Starch, 1 Milk	2 Starch, 1 Milk	3 Starch, 1 Milk

FRIDAY

	1500 calories	1800 calories	2000 calories
BREAKFAST	**Breakfast Casserole,** *page 167,* 1 serving Grits, ½ c Light butter, 1 tbsp Grapefruit, ½	**Breakfast Casserole,** *page 167,* 1 serving Grits, ½ c Light butter, 1 tbsp Grapefruit, ½	**Breakfast Casserole,** *page 167,* 1 serving Grits, 1 c Light butter, 2 tbsp Grapefruit, ½ Fat-free milk, 1 c
	2 Starch, 1 Fruit, 3 Meat, 1 Fat	2 Starch, 1 Fruit, 3 Meat, 1 Fat	3 Starch, 1 Fruit, 3 Meat, 1 Milk, 2 Fat
LUNCH	**Stuffed Peppers,** *page 81,* 1 serving Crisp breadsticks, 4 Red grapes, 1 c	**Stuffed Peppers,** *page 81,* 1 serving Crisp breadsticks, 4 Red grapes, 1 c	**Stuffed Peppers,** *page 81,* 1 serving Crisp breadsticks, 8 Red grapes, 1 c
	2½ Starch, 2 Veg, 1 Fruit, 1 Meat	2½ Starch, 2 Veg, 1 Fruit, 1 Meat	3½ Starch, 2 Veg, 1 Fruit, 1 Meat
DINNER	**Veal Parmigiana,** *page 87,* 1 serving Angel hair pasta, ½ c Spinach salad, 1 c Reduced-fat olive oil vinaigrette, 1 tbsp Sliced pear, 1	**Veal Parmigiana,** *page 87,* 1 serving Angel hair pasta, 1 c Spinach salad, 1 c Reduced-fat olive oil vinaigrette, 1 tbsp Sliced pear, 1	**Veal Parmigiana,** *page 87,* 1 serving Angel hair pasta, 1 c Spinach salad, 2 c Reduced-fat olive oil vinaigrette, 2 tbsp Sliced pear, 1
	2 Starch, 1 Veg, 1 Fruit, 3½ Meat, 2 Fat	3 Starch, 1 Veg, 1 Fruit, 3½ Meat, 1 Fat	3 Starch, 2 Veg, 1 Fruit, 3½ Meat, 2 Fat
SNACK	**Chocolate-Peppermint Parfaits,** *page 51,* 1 serving	**Chocolate-Peppermint Parfaits,** *page 51,* 1 serving	**Chocolate-Peppermint Parfaits,** *page 51,* 1 serving Fat-free milk, 1 c
	2 Starch	2 Starch	2 Starch, 1 Milk

Abbreviations Key: **tbsp** = tablespoon(s) **tsp** = teaspoon(s) **oz** = ounce(s) **c** = cup(s)

SATURDAY

Buttermilk Biscuits,
page 34,
2 biscuits
Light butter, 1 tbsp
Scrambled egg, 1
Orange juice, ½ c

2 Starch, 1 Fruit,
1 Meat, 1 Fat

Buttermilk Biscuits,
page 34,
2 biscuits
Light butter, 1 tbsp
Scrambled egg, 1
Orange juice, ½ c

2 Starch, 1 Fruit,
1 Meat, 1 Fat

Buttermilk Biscuits,
page 34,
3 biscuits
Light butter, 2 tbsp
Scrambled egg, 2
Orange juice, ½ c

3 Starch, 1 Fruit,
2 Meat, 2 Fat

Grilled Cheese Sandwiches Deluxe,
page 157,
1 serving
Celery sticks, 1 c
Reduced-fat ranch dressing, 1 tbsp
Apple, 1

3 Starch, 1 Veg,
1 Fruit, 1 Meat,
1 Milk, 1 Fat

Grilled Cheese Sandwiches Deluxe,
page 157,
1 serving
Fresh Tomato Soup, *page 146,*
1 serving
Celery sticks, 1 c
Reduced-fat ranch dressing, 2 tbsp

3 Starch, 4 Veg,
1 Fruit, 1 Milk,
1 Meat, 2 Fat

Grilled Cheese Sandwiches Deluxe,
page 157,
1 serving
Fresh Tomato Soup, *page 146,*
1 serving
Celery sticks, 1 c
Reduced-fat ranch dressing, 2 tbsp

3 Starch, 4 Veg,
1 Fruit, 1 Milk,
1 Meat, 2 Fat

Country-Style Pork Chops,
page 88,
1 serving
Garden Potato Salad,
page 119,
1 serving
Green beans, ½ c
Watermelon cubes, 1¼ c

2 Starch, 2 Veg,
1 Fruit, 3½ Meat

Country-Style Pork Chops,
page 88,
1 serving
Garden Potato Salad,
page 119,
1 serving
Green beans, ½ c
Whole wheat roll, 1
Light butter, 1 tbsp
Watermelon cubes, 1¼ c

3 Starch, 2 Veg,
1 Fruit, 3½ Meat,
1 Fat

Country-Style Pork Chops,
page 88,
1 serving
Garden Potato Salad,
page 119,
1 serving
Green beans, ½ c
Whole wheat rolls, 2
Light butter, 1 tbsp
Watermelon cubes, 1¼ c

4 Starch, 2 Veg,
1 Fruit, 3½ Meat,
1 Fat

Air-popped popcorn, 3 c
Sugar-free hot cocoa, 1 c

1 Starch, 1 Milk

Air-popped popcorn, 6 c
Sugar-free hot cocoa, 1 c

2 Starch, 1 Milk

Air-popped popcorn, 6 c
Sugar-free hot cocoa, 1 c

2 Starch, 1 Milk

SUNDAY

Shredded Wheat Pancakes,
page 37,
2 pancakes
Sugar-free syrup, 2 tbsp
Strawberries, 1¼ c
Fat-free milk, 1 c

2 Starch, 1 Fruit,
1 Milk, 1 Fat

Shredded Wheat Pancakes,
page 37,
2 pancakes
Light butter, 2 tbsp
Sugar-free syrup, 2 tbsp
Strawberries, 1¼ c
Fat-free milk, 1 c

2 Starch, 1 Fruit,
1 Milk, 3 Fat

Shredded Wheat Pancakes,
page 37,
3 pancakes
Light butter, 2 tbsp
Sugar-free syrup, 2 tbsp
Strawberries, 1¼ c
Fat-free milk, 1 c

3 Starch, 1 Fruit,
1 Milk, 3½ Fat

Chicken Tenders Salad,
page 121,
1 serving
Whole wheat crackers, 5
Orange, 1

3 Starch, 1 Veg,
1 Fruit, 4 Meat,
1 Fat

Chicken Tenders Salad,
page 121,
1 serving
Whole wheat crackers, 10
Orange, 1

4 Starch, 1 Veg,
1 Fruit, 4 Meat,
1 Fat

Chicken Tenders Salad,
page 121,
1 serving
Whole wheat crackers, 10
Orange, 1

4 Starch, 1 Veg,
1 Fruit, 4 Meat,
1 Fat

Vegetable Lasagna,
page 170,
1 serving
Mixed green salad, 1 c
Low-fat vinaigrette, 2 tbsp
Melon balls, 1 c

2 Starch, 1 Veg,
1 Fruit, 2 Meat,
1 Fat

Vegetable Lasagna,
page 170,
1 serving
Mixed green salad, 2 c
Low-fat vinaigrette, 4 tbsp
French bread, 1 slice
Melon balls, 1 c

3 Starch, 2 Veg,
1 Fruit, 2 Meat,
2 Fat

Vegetable Lasagna,
page 170,
1 serving
Mixed green salad, 2 c
Low-fat vinaigrette, 4 tbsp
French bread, 2 slices
Melon balls, 1 c

4 Starch, 2 Veg,
1 Fruit, 2 Meat,
2 Fat

Banana Pudding,
page 10,
1 serving

1 Starch, 1 Fruit,
1 Fat

Banana Pudding,
page 10,
1 serving

1 Starch, 1 Fruit,
1 Fat

Banana Pudding,
page 10,
1 serving

1 Starch, 1 Fruit,
1 Fat

SUGAR SUBSTITUTE GUIDE

Sugar Substitute*	Description	Amount to equal ½ cup sugar
THE FOLLOWING SUGAR SUBSTITUTES ARE MEASURED LIKE SUGAR, SO TO REPLACE SUGAR IN RECIPES, USE THE SAME AMOUNT OF SUBSTITUTE AS YOU WOULD OF SUGAR.		
DiabetiSweet	Contains a combination of acesulfame-K and isomalt; no aftertaste; looks like sugar; heat stable	½ cup
Equal Spoonful	Contains aspartame; no aftertaste; loses some sweetness in high heat	½ cup
Splenda	Contains sucralose, a modified sugar molecule that is not absorbed by the body; no aftertaste; extremely heat stable; also available in packets	½ cup
Sugar Twin	Contains saccharin; some aftertaste; heat stable	½ cup
THESE SUGAR SUBSTITUTES ARE CONCENTRATED, SO USE THESE SMALLER MEASURES IN PLACE OF ½ CUP SUGAR TO GET THE SAME SWEETNESS.		
Equal for Recipes	Contains aspartame; no aftertaste; the bulk form of Equal packets; loses some sweetness in high heat	3½ teaspoons
Equal Packets	Contains aspartame; no aftertaste; same as Equal for Recipes (above), but in packets; loses some sweetness in high heat	12 packets
Sweet 'N Low	Contains saccharin; some aftertaste; available in bulk form or in packets; heat stable	1 tablespoon or 12 packets
Sweet One	Contains acesulfame-K; no aftertaste; heat stable	12 packets
LIQUID SUGAR SUBSTITUTES BLEND EASILY WITH OTHER INGREDIENTS AND WORK WELL IN SAUCES AND MARINADES.		
Sweet 'N Low	Contains saccharin; some aftertaste; heat stable	1 tablespoon
Sweet-10	Contains saccharin; some aftertaste; heat stable	1 tablespoon

*This list includes the sugar substitutes that we use most often in our Test Kitchens. It is not an inclusive list and is not meant as an endorsement of any particular product.

BEVERAGES & SNACKS

Summertime Lemonade, page 22

Summertime Lemonade • Holiday Tea Mix • Sugar-Free Cocoa Mix
Fat-Free Eggnog • Cheese Wafers • Homemade Peanut Butter
Deviled Eggs • Cucumber Tea Sandwiches • Sausage-Cheese Balls

Prep: 12 minutes

Summertime Lemonade

*Minted Lemonade:
Add 2 tablespoons
fresh mint leaves to
hot lemon juice
mixture. Let stand
10 minutes. Strain
mixture, discarding
mint.*

5   cups water
1½ cups fresh lemon juice (about 10 large lemons)
½   cup "measures-like-sugar" calorie-free sweetener

Combine water and lemon juice in a large nonaluminum saucepan;
bring to a boil.
Remove from heat. Stir in sweetener. Cover and chill. Serve over ice.
Yield: 6 (1-cup) servings.

Per Serving:

Calories 24	Fiber 0.0g
Fat 0.0g (sat 0.0g)	Cholesterol 0mg
Protein 0.2g	Sodium 1mg
Carbohydrate 7.0g	Exchange ½ Fruit

(Photograph on page 21)

Sugar Substitutes
If you use packets of calorie-free sweetener instead of a
"measures-like-sugar" brand, here are some helpful conversions:

Sugar	"Measures-like-sugar" calorie-free sweetener	Packets of calorie-free sweetener	
2 teaspoons	2 teaspoons	1	packet (¼ teaspoon)
1 tablespoon	1 tablespoon	1½	packets (½ teaspoon)
¼ cup	¼ cup	6	packets (1¾ teaspoons)
½ cup	½ cup	12	packets (3½ teaspoons)
1 cup	1 cup	24	packets (7¼ teaspoons)

Prep: 5 minutes

Holiday Tea Mix

make
ahead

super
quick

1¼ cups "measures-like-sugar" calorie-free sweetener
1 (1.8-ounce) container sugar-free orange drink mix (such as
       sugar-free Tang)
1 (0.45-ounce) package sugar-free lemonade mix
¾ cup unsweetened instant tea without lemon
1 teaspoon ground cloves
2 teaspoons ground cinnamon

Combine all ingredients in a large bowl; stir well. Store in an airtight container.

To serve, spoon 2 teaspoons tea mix into each cup. Add ¾ cup boiling water, and stir well. **Yield:** 54 (¾-cup) servings.

Per Serving:

Calories 8	Fiber 0.0g
Fat 0.0g (sat 0.0g)	Cholesterol 0mg
Protein 0.1g	Sodium 7mg
Carbohydrate 1.7g	Exchange Free

Gift Idea:
This spiced tea mix is a great gift idea. Spoon the mix (one recipe makes 2¼ cups of mix) into a decorative jar or canister, attach the recipe, and tie a ribbon on the container.

Prep: 5 minutes

Sugar-Free Cocoa Mix

Got Calcium?:

If you're not a milk drinker, hot cocoa is a great way to add calcium to your diet. One serving of this sugar-free cocoa has 166mg of calcium. Most adults need 1,000mg per day. Women over 51 years of age need 1,200mg per day.

2⅓ cups instant nonfat dry milk
⅓   cup unsweetened cocoa
⅓   cup "measures-like-sugar" calorie-free sweetener
Miniature marshmallows (optional)
Sugar-free candy canes (optional)

Combine first 3 ingredients in a large bowl; stir well. Store in an air-tight container.

To serve, spoon ¼ cup cocoa mix into each mug. Add 1 cup boiling water, and stir well. Top with miniature marshmallows or sugar-free candy canes, if desired. **Yield:** 12 (1-cup) servings.

Per Serving:

Calories 62	Fiber 0.8g
Fat 0.4g (sat 0.3g)	Cholesterol 2mg
Protein 5.1g	Sodium 73mg
Carbohydrate 13.5g	Exchange 1 Skim Milk

Prep: 5 minutes

Fat-Free Eggnog

5¾ cups fat-free half-and-half
1   teaspoon vanilla extract
1   teaspoon rum flavoring
1   (1-ounce) package sugar-free, fat-free vanilla instant pudding mix
1   tablespoon "measures-like-sugar" calorie-free sweetener
7   tablespoons frozen fat-free whipped topping, thawed
Ground nutmeg (optional)

Combine half-and-half, vanilla, and rum flavoring in a large bowl.
Combine pudding mix and sweetener in a small bowl. Add pudding mixture to half-and-half mixture, stirring with a wire whisk until smooth. Cover and chill until ready to serve.
To serve, top each serving with 1 tablespoon whipped topping. Sprinkle with nutmeg, if desired. **Yield:** 7 (¾-cup) servings.

Note: Fat-free half-and-half usually comes in 1-pint cartons. You'll need to buy three cartons to get 5¾ cups.

Per Serving:

Calories 159
Fat 0.0g (sat 0.0g)
Protein 3.3g
Carbohydrate 25.0g
Fiber 0.0g
Cholesterol 0mg
Sodium 388mg
Exchanges 1½ Starch

Prep: 20 minutes   Cook: 15 minutes per batch

Cheese Wafers

¼   cup margarine, softened
1   cup (4 ounces) shredded reduced-fat sharp Cheddar cheese
¼   cup low-fat buttermilk
1½   cups crisp rice cereal
1   cup all-purpose flour
⅛   teaspoon salt
⅛   teaspoon ground red pepper
Dash of paprika

Preheat oven to 350°.

Place margarine, cheese, and buttermilk in a food processor; process until blended, stopping once to scrape down sides. Add cereal and remaining 4 ingredients; process until mixture forms a ball, stopping often to scrape down sides.

Shape dough into ½-inch balls. Place balls about 2 inches apart on ungreased baking sheets. Flatten each ball in a crisscross pattern with a fork dipped in flour. Bake at 350° for 15 minutes or until lightly browned. Remove wafers from pans; cool completely on wire racks.

Yield: 18 servings (serving size: 3 wafers).

Say Cheese: Reduced-fat Cheddar cheese has 5 grams of fat per 1-ounce serving compared to about 8 grams of fat for regular Cheddar cheese. For this recipe, be sure to use a reduced-fat cheese instead of a fat-free product.

Per Serving:

Calories 76	Fiber 0.2g
Fat 3.8g (sat 1.5g)	Cholesterol 5mg
Protein 3.0g	Sodium 122mg
Carbohydrate 7.5g	Exchanges ½ Starch, 1 Fat

Homemade Peanut Butter

1 pound unshelled, unsalted roasted peanuts (2½ cups shelled)

Shell peanuts; remove and discard skins. Place peanuts in a food processor. Process 3 minutes, stopping once to scrape down sides. Store in refrigerator. **Yield:** 1¼ cups (serving size: 2 tablespoons).

Note: The natural oil in the peanuts may rise to the top of the jar. Stir the oil back into the peanut butter before using.

Peanut Pointers:
We like the flavor of unsalted peanuts, but if salt isn't a problem for you, you can make this peanut butter with salted peanuts. And, to save time, you can start with shelled roasted peanuts.

Per Serving:

Calories 192	Fiber 2.6g
Fat 16.4g (sat 2.3g)	Cholesterol 0mg
Protein 7.8g	Sodium 2mg
Carbohydrate 7.0g	Exchanges 1 High-Fat Meat, 1½ Fat

What's in the Jar?

Although the calories, carbohydrate, and fat in homemade peanut butter are not that different from store-bought versions, the sodium is much lower. Plus you get much more of a natural "peanutty" flavor with the homemade. Compare the nutrients in these different types of peanut butter:

Peanut Butter (2 tablespoons)	Calories	Carbs	Fat	Sodium
Homemade	192	7.0g	16.4g	2mg
No-sugar-added *(Fifty-50)*	220	6.0g	18.0g	15mg
Reduced-fat, creamy *(Jif)*	190	15.0g	12.0g	250mg
Reduced-fat, crunchy *(Jif)*	190	15.0g	12.0g	250mg
Regular, creamy *(Jif)*	190	7.0g	16.0g	150mg
Regular, crunchy *(Jif)*	190	7.0g	16.0g	150mg

Prep: 4 minutes   Cook: 20 minutes

Deviled Eggs

6   hard-cooked large eggs, peeled
2½ tablespoons low-fat mayonnaise
1   tablespoon sweet pickle relish, drained
1   tablespoon grated onion
1   teaspoon prepared mustard
⅛   teaspoon salt
Dash of ground white pepper
Paprika

Slice eggs in half lengthwise. Scoop out yolks, and place 4 yolks in a small bowl. (Reserve remaining yolks for another use.) Set whites aside.

Mash yolks with a fork. Add mayonnaise, pickle relish, onion, mustard, salt, and pepper; stir well.

Spoon mixture evenly into egg whites; sprinkle with paprika. **Yield:** 12 servings (serving size: 1 egg half).

Per Serving:

Calories 39	Fiber 0.0g
Fat 2.6g (sat 0.5g)	Cholesterol 74mg
Protein 2.7g	Sodium 90mg
Carbohydrate 1.1g	Exchange ½ Medium-Fat Meat

Prep: 30 minutes

Cucumber Tea Sandwiches

1   (8-ounce) carton plain fat-free yogurt
1/3 cup light cream cheese
1   cup shredded seeded peeled cucumber
3   tablespoons shredded onion
1/8 teaspoon salt
16 (1-ounce) slices white sandwich bread
16 (1-ounce) slices whole wheat bread
32 thin cucumber slices
Parsley sprigs (optional)

Tea Time:
Put these bite-size party sandwiches on the menu the next time you host a shower or tea.

Spoon yogurt onto several layers of heavy-duty paper towels, spreading to 1/2-inch thickness. Cover with additional paper towels; let stand 5 minutes.

Combine yogurt and cream cheese, stirring until smooth. Press shredded cucumber and onion between paper towels to remove excess moisture. Stir vegetables and salt into yogurt mixture.

Cut 2 (1¾-inch) rounds out of each bread slice, using a cookie cutter. Spread 1½ teaspoons yogurt mixture on one side of each of 16 white bread rounds; top each with a cucumber slice and a whole wheat round. Repeat procedure, spreading yogurt mixture on 16 whole wheat rounds, and topping each with a cucumber slice and a white bread round. Reserve remaining yogurt mixture.

Transfer sandwiches to a platter. Cover and chill until ready to serve. Dollop remaining yogurt mixture on sandwiches. Garnish with parsley sprigs, if desired. **Yield:** 32 sandwiches.

Per Sandwich:

Calories 47	Fiber 0.6g
Fat 0.9g (sat 0.3g)	Cholesterol 2mg
Protein 2.1g	Sodium 102mg
Carbohydrate 8.1g	Exchange 1/2 Starch

Sausage-Cheese Balls

½   pound turkey breakfast sausage
1   cup (4 ounces) shredded reduced-fat sharp Cheddar cheese
3   tablespoons chopped fresh parsley
¼   teaspoon ground red pepper
1¼ cups low-fat baking mix (such as reduced-fat Bisquick)
Cooking spray

Preheat oven to 350°.

Combine sausage, cheese, parsley, and pepper in a medium bowl, stirring well. Add baking mix, and mix well.

Coat a baking sheet with cooking spray. Shape meat mixture into 1-inch balls; place balls on baking sheet and lightly coat with cooking spray. Bake at 350° for 20 to 25 minutes or until done. Serve warm.

Yield: 12 servings (serving size: 2 balls).

Per Serving:

Calories 122	Fiber 0.4g
Fat 6.6g (sat 1.2g)	Cholesterol 22mg
Protein 6.6g	Sodium 360mg
Carbohydrate 9.0g	Exchanges ½ Starch, 1 Lean Meat

BREADS

Buttermilk Biscuits, page 34

Buttermilk Biscuits • Easy Drop Biscuits • Shredded Wheat Pancakes
Blueberry Muffins • Corn Bread • Broccoli Corn Bread
Peppered Spoonbread • Banana Bread • Cheddar Cheese Loaf
Cinnamon Rolls • Butter Crescent Rolls

Buttermilk Biscuits

Cooking Secret:
Handle dough with
a light touch for
fluffy biscuits.
Biscuit dough
should be slightly
sticky and should
be kneaded gently.
Take care to keep
the cutter straight
as you cut the
dough; the biscuits
will rise evenly if
you do.

2	cups all-purpose flour
2½	teaspoons baking powder
¼	teaspoon baking soda
¼	teaspoon salt
2	teaspoons sugar
3	tablespoons chilled reduced-calorie stick margarine, cut into small pieces
¾	cup low-fat buttermilk

Fat-free butter spray (such as I Can't Believe It's Not Butter!)
Low-sugar jelly (optional)

Preheat oven to 425°.

Lightly spoon flour into dry measuring cups; level with a knife. Combine flour and next 4 ingredients in a medium bowl; cut in margarine with a pastry blender or 2 knives until mixture resembles coarse meal. Add buttermilk, stirring just until moist.

Turn dough out onto a lightly floured surface, and knead 10 to 12 times. Roll dough to a ½-inch thickness; cut into rounds with a 2-inch biscuit cutter.

Place rounds on an ungreased baking sheet. Bake at 425° for 10 minutes or until golden. Lightly spray biscuits with butter spray. Serve with low-sugar jelly, if desired. **Yield:** 16 biscuits.

Per Biscuit:

Calories 75	Fiber 0.4g
Fat 1.6g (sat 0.1g)	Cholesterol 0mg
Protein 2.0g	Sodium 167mg
Carbohydrate 13.2g	Exchange 1 Starch

(Photograph on page 33)

Prep: 10 minutes   Cook: 15 minutes

Easy Drop Biscuits

1½ cups all-purpose flour
2   teaspoons baking powder
½   teaspoon baking soda
¼   teaspoon salt
1   cup plain low-fat yogurt
¼   cup egg substitute
1   tablespoon vegetable oil
Cooking spray

Preheat oven to 400°.

Lightly spoon flour into dry measuring cups; level with a knife. Combine flour and next 3 ingredients; make a well in center of mixture. Combine yogurt, egg substitute, and oil; add to flour mixture, stirring just until moist.

Drop dough by rounded tablespoonfuls, 2 inches apart, onto a baking sheet coated with cooking spray. Bake at 400° for 15 minutes or until golden. **Yield:** 1 dozen.

Per Biscuit:

Calories 82	Fiber 0.4g
Fat 1.6g (sat 0.4g)	Cholesterol 1mg
Protein 3.1g	Sodium 154mg
Carbohydrate 13.5g	Exchange 1 Starch

Low-Sugar Jelly:

If you want to serve your biscuits with jelly, check out all of the flavors of low-sugar jellies and jams at the supermarket. Or turn to page 13 for some recipes and tips for making your own.

Prep: 5 minutes   Cook: 3 minutes per batch

Shredded Wheat Pancakes

¾   cup all-purpose flour
½   cup crushed shredded whole wheat cereal biscuits
1   tablespoon baking powder
2   teaspoons "measures-like sugar" calorie-free sweetener
¼   teaspoon salt
1   large egg, beaten
1   cup fat-free milk
1   tablespoon vegetable oil

Fiber Fact:
Adding crushed
whole wheat cereal
to the batter adds
fiber to these
pancakes and gives
them a hearty,
nutty flavor.

Preheat griddle or skillet.

Lightly spoon flour into dry measuring cups; level with a knife. Combine flour and next 4 ingredients in a medium bowl; make a well in center of mixture. Combine egg, milk, and oil; add to dry ingredients, stirring just until moist.

For each pancake, spoon about ¼ cup batter onto a hot nonstick griddle or skillet. Turn pancakes when tops are covered with bubbles and edges look cooked. **Yield:** 8 (4-inch) pancakes.

Per Pancake:

Calories 90	**Fiber** 0.6g
Fat 2.6g (sat 0.4g)	**Cholesterol** 28mg
Protein 3.4g	**Sodium** 98mg
Carbohydrate 13.2g	**Exchanges** 1 Starch, ½ Fat

Favorite Pancake Toppers

Don't forget to count the carbs in your favorite pancake topper.

Reduced-sugar jelly	1 tablespoon	9 grams carbohydrate
Fruit spread	1 tablespoon	10 grams carbohydrate
Light butter	1 tablespoon	0 grams carbohydrate
Sugar-free syrup	1 tablespoon	2 grams carbohydrate

Blueberry Muffins

Bring on the
Blueberries:
There's some
promising new
research showing
that eating
blueberries may
improve brain
function and slow
the memory loss
that sometimes
occurs with aging.

⅔ cup all-purpose flour, divided
⅓ cup fresh or frozen blueberries, thawed
½ teaspoon baking powder
¼ teaspoon baking soda
⅛ teaspoon salt
3 tablespoons "measures-like-sugar" calorie-free sweetener
⅓ cup plain fat-free yogurt
2 teaspoons vegetable oil
½ teaspoon vanilla extract
1 large egg white, lightly beaten
Cooking spray

Preheat oven to 375°.

Lightly spoon flour into dry measuring cups; level with a knife. Toss blueberries with 2 teaspoons flour, and set aside. Combine remaining flour, baking powder, and next 3 ingredients in a medium bowl; make a well in center of mixture. Combine yogurt and next 3 ingredients; add to dry ingredients, stirring just until moist. Fold blueberries into batter.

Spoon batter evenly into 4 muffin cups coated with cooking spray. Bake at 375° for 18 minutes. Remove from pan immediately, and cool on a wire rack. **Yield:** 4 muffins.

Per Muffin:

Calories 132	**Fiber** 0.9g
Fat 2.5g (sat 0.2g)	**Cholesterol** 0mg
Protein 3.9g	**Sodium** 239mg
Carbohydrate 28.5g	**Exchanges** 1 Starch, 1 Fruit

Prep: 10 minutes   Cook: 20 minutes

Corn Bread

¾   cup all-purpose flour
1¼   cups yellow cornmeal
2   teaspoons baking powder
½   teaspoon baking soda
¼   teaspoon salt
1   tablespoon sugar
1   cup low-fat buttermilk
1   (8.5-ounce) can cream-style corn
1   large egg, lightly beaten
Cooking spray

Add Flavor:

For a spicy flavor option, add 3 tablespoons minced jalapeño pepper (about 3 small) and ½ cup sliced green onions to the batter.

Preheat oven to 425°.

Lightly spoon flour into dry measuring cups; level with a knife. Combine flour, cornmeal, and next 4 ingredients in a bowl; stir well.

Combine buttermilk, corn, and egg in a small bowl; stir well. Add to cornmeal mixture, stirring just until moist. Pour batter into an 8-inch square baking pan coated with cooking spray. Bake at 425° for 20 to 22 minutes or until golden. Cool 5 minutes in pan on a wire rack. Remove from pan and cut into squares. Serve warm. **Yield:** 9 servings (serving size: 1 square).

Per Serving:

Calories 145	Fiber 2.6g
Fat 1.6g (sat 0.4g)	Cholesterol 25mg
Protein 4.6g	Sodium 367mg
Carbohydrate 28.6g	Exchanges 2 Starch

Broccoli Corn Bread

Stock Up:

To make an extra pan of corn bread to freeze and have on hand for later, use the whole package of broccoli and double the rest of the ingredients.

Cool the extra bread on a wire rack, then wrap in heavy-duty aluminum foil. Freeze up to 2 weeks. Thaw in refrigerator and bake, covered loosely, at 400° for 20 minutes or until thoroughly heated.

Cooking spray
1   tablespoon reduced-calorie margarine
½   (10-ounce) package frozen chopped broccoli, thawed and
         drained
1   (8½-ounce) package corn muffin mix
¾   cup 1% low-fat cottage cheese
½   cup egg substitute
½   cup finely chopped onion
1   (2-ounce) jar diced pimiento, drained
¼   teaspoon cracked pepper

Preheat oven to 350°.

Coat an 8-inch square baking pan with cooking spray. Add margarine, and place in a 350° oven for 3 minutes or until margarine melts.

Press broccoli between paper towels to remove excess moisture. Combine broccoli, muffin mix and remaining 5 ingredients, stirring well. Spoon into prepared pan. Bake at 350° for 1 hour or until golden.

Yield: 16 servings (serving size: 1 square).

Per Serving:

Calories 82	Fiber 0.9g
Fat 2.2g (sat 0.7g)	Cholesterol 0mg
Protein 3.4g	Sodium 186mg
Carbohydrate 12.2g	Exchange 1 Starch

Peppered Spoonbread

Egg Info:

One-fourth cup of egg substitute is the equivalent of one egg, but has 0 grams of fat compared to 5 grams for a whole egg.

1½ cups low-fat buttermilk
¾ cup water
¾ cup yellow cornmeal
1 tablespoon reduced-calorie margarine
¾ teaspoon cracked pepper
¼ teaspoon salt
2 large egg whites
¼ cup egg substitute
Cooking spray

Preheat oven to 350°.

Combine first 6 ingredients in a medium saucepan; cook over medium heat 5 minutes or until thick, stirring constantly. Remove from heat.

Beat egg whites with a mixer at high speed until stiff peaks form. With mixer running, slowly add egg substitute. Gradually stir about one-third of hot cornmeal mixture into egg mixture; add to remaining hot cornmeal mixture, stirring constantly. Pour into a 1½-quart soufflé dish coated with cooking spray. Bake at 350° for 25 to 30 minutes or until lightly browned. Serve immediately. **Yield:** 6 servings (serving size: about 1 cup).

Per Serving:

Calories 114	Fiber 1.4g
Fat 2.2g (sat 0.7g)	Cholesterol 4mg
Protein 6.2g	Sodium 223mg
Carbohydrate 17.0g	Exchanges 1 Starch, ½ Fat

Prep: 10 minutes   Cook: 1 hour

Banana Bread

1½   cups all-purpose flour
¼   cup sugar
2   teaspoons baking powder
1   teaspoon baking soda
½   teaspoon salt
½   cup wheat germ
1   cup mashed ripe banana (about 3 medium bananas)
¼   cup plain fat-free yogurt
2   tablespoons vegetable oil
4   large egg whites, lightly beaten
Cooking spray

Preheat oven to 350°.

Lightly spoon flour into dry measuring cups; level with a knife. Combine flour and next 5 ingredients in a large bowl; stir well. Stir together banana and yogurt. Add oil and egg whites; stir well. Add banana mixture to flour mixture, stirring just until moist. Spoon batter into an 8 x 4-inch loaf pan coated with cooking spray.

Bake at 350° for 1 hour or until a wooden pick inserted in center comes out clean. Cool 10 minutes in pan on a wire rack; remove from pan. Cool completely on wire rack. **Yield:** 16 servings (serving size: 1 slice).

Per Slice:

Calories 102	Fiber 1.1g
Fat 2.3g (sat 0.2g)	Cholesterol 0mg
Protein 3.4g	Sodium 229mg
Carbohydrate 17.7g	Exchanges 1 Starch, ½ Fat

Wheat Germ Benefits:
This banana bread boasts extra benefits because it contains wheat germ, a good source of vitamin E. Vitamin E may help prevent blood clots, protect against strokes, reduce the risk of cancer, and may protect against cataracts.

Cheddar Cheese Loaf

3¾ cups low-fat baking mix (such as reduced-fat Bisquick)
¾ cup (3 ounces) shredded reduced-fat sharp Cheddar cheese
1½ cups fat-free milk
¼ cup egg substitute
⅛ to ¼ teaspoon ground red pepper
Cooking spray

Try Swiss:

For a flavor variation, you can make this bread with shredded reduced-fat Swiss cheese.

Preheat oven to 350°.

Combine baking mix and cheese. Add milk, egg substitute, and pepper, stirring 2 minutes or until blended. Spoon into a 9 x 5-inch loaf pan coated with cooking spray. Bake at 350° for 45 minutes. Cool 10 minutes in pan on a wire rack; remove from pan. Cool completely on wire rack. **Yield:** 18 (½-inch-thick) slices.

Per Serving:

Calories 157	Fiber 0.9g
Fat 3.5g (sat 0.5g)	Cholesterol 2mg
Protein 6.0g	Sodium 534mg
Carbohydrate 27.0g	Exchanges 2 Starch

Say "Cheese"!

Compare the fat and calorie contents of several types of cheese:

Cheese	Fat (grams)	Calories
Cheddar (1 ounce)	9.4	114
Cheddar, 2% reduced-fat (1 ounce)	6.1	91
Mozzarella, part skim (1 ounce)	4.9	79
Monterey Jack (1 ounce)	8.6	106
Parmesan (1 ounce)	7.3	111
Swiss (1 ounce)	7.8	106
Swiss, reduced-fat (1 ounce)	6.1	91

Prep: 50 minutes   Stand: 1 hour 35 minutes   Cook: 22 minutes

Cinnamon Rolls

Half the Fat:

These sweet and tender homemade cinnamon rolls have about half the fat of packaged bakery cinnamon rolls and about 10 grams less carbohydrate.

1	cup fat-free milk
3	tablespoons sugar
1	tablespoon margarine
1	package dry yeast
¼	cup warm water (100° to 110°)
1	large egg, lightly beaten
1	teaspoon salt
4	cups bread flour, divided

Cooking spray

2	tablespoons margarine, melted
⅓	cup "measures-like-sugar" brown sugar calorie-free sweetener
2	teaspoons ground cinnamon
6	tablespoons "measures-like-sugar" calorie-free sweetener
2	tablespoons fat-free milk

Heat 1 cup milk over medium-high heat in a heavy saucepan to 180° or until tiny bubbles form around edge (do not boil). Remove from heat; add 3 tablespoons sugar and 1 tablespoon margarine; stir until margarine melts. Cool to 105° to 115°.

Combine yeast and warm water; let stand 5 minutes. Combine milk mixture, yeast mixture, egg, and salt in a large bowl; stir well. Lightly spoon flour into dry measuring cups; level with a knife. Gradually stir in 3¾ cups flour to make a soft dough.

Turn dough out onto a lightly floured surface; knead until smooth and elastic (about 8 minutes). Add enough remaining flour, 1 tablespoon at a time, to keep dough from sticking to surface. Place dough in a bowl coated with cooking spray, turning to coat top. Cover and let rise in a warm place (85°), free from drafts, 1 hour or until doubled in size.

Punch dough down. Turn out onto a floured surface; roll into a 20 x 8-inch rectangle. Brush with 2 tablespoons melted margarine. Combine brown sugar sweetener and cinnamon; sprinkle over dough.

Roll up dough, starting at long side, pressing firmly to eliminate air pockets; pinch seam to seal (do not seal ends).

Cut into 20 (1-inch) slices, using clean dental floss. Place slices in a 13 x 9-inch baking pan coated with cooking spray. Cover; let rise in a warm place, free from drafts, 30 minutes or until doubled in size. Preheat oven to 350°. Bake at 350° for 22 minutes or until done.

Combine sweetener substitute and 2 tablespoons milk; stir well. Drizzle over warm rolls. **Yield:** 20 rolls.

Per Roll:

Calories 135	Fiber 0.2g
Fat 2.5g (sat 0.5g)	Cholesterol 11mg
Protein 4.2g	Sodium 152mg
Carbohydrate 23.9g	Exchanges 1½ Starch, ½ Fat

Prep: 30 minutes   Stand: 1 hour 35 minutes   Cook: 12 minutes

Butter Crescent Rolls

Test Kitchen Secret:
Buttery-tasting
crescent rolls
without butter?
Pretty darn close.
Using yogurt in
the dough and
coating the rolls
with butter-flavored
cooking spray gives
them an extra-rich
flavor.

1   package dry yeast
¼   cup warm water (100° to 110°)
¼   cup sugar
½   cup plain fat-free yogurt
3   tablespoons margarine, melted
2   large egg whites, lightly beaten
¾   teaspoon salt
3¼   cups all-purpose flour
Butter-flavored cooking spray

Combine yeast and warm water in a 1-cup liquid measuring cup; let stand 5 minutes.

Combine yeast mixture, sugar, and next 4 ingredients in a large bowl, stirring until blended. Gradually stir in enough flour to make a soft dough. Turn dough out onto a lightly floured surface, and knead 3 or 4 times. Place in a bowl coated with cooking spray, turning to coat top. Cover and let rise in a warm place (85°), free from drafts, 1 hour or until doubled in size.

Punch dough down, and divide into thirds; shape each portion into a ball. Roll each ball into a 12-inch circle on a lightly floured surface; coat lightly with cooking spray. Cut each circle into 12 wedges. Roll up each wedge, starting with wide end; place rolls, point sides down, on baking sheets coated with cooking spray.

Cover and let rise in a warm place (85°), free from drafts, 30 minutes or until doubled in size. Preheat oven to 375°. Bake at 375° for 12 minutes or until golden. Serve immediately. **Yield:** 3 dozen.

Per Roll:

Calories 59	Fiber 0.4g
Fat 1.1g (sat 0.2g)	Cholesterol 0mg
Protein 1.6g	Sodium 65mg
Carbohydrate 10.3g	Exchange 1 Starch

DESSERTS

Homestyle Apple Pie, page 65

Chocolate Milkshake • Chocolate-Peppermint Parfaits

Butter Pecan Ice Cream • Chocolate Chip Cookies

Oatmeal-Raisin Cookies • Strawberry Shortcakes • Raisin-Date Cake

Vanilla Pound Cake • Chocolate Marbled Pound Cake

Chocolate-Peanut Butter Bread Pudding • Blackberry Cobbler

Homestyle Apple Pie • Cherry Pie

Prep: 5 minutes

Chocolate Milkshake

Nutrition Note:
Some new research
shows that eating
low-fat calcium-
containing foods
may help you burn
fat. Because it has
both milk and ice
cream, this shake is
a yummy way to get
your calcium. One
serving provides
173 milligrams of
calcium, which is
about 14 percent
of the daily
requirement for
men and women
over 50 years
of age.

1½ cups vanilla fat-free, no-sugar-added ice cream
¾   cup fat-free milk
1   tablespoon no-sugar-added chocolate drink mix
1   tablespoon sugar-free chocolate syrup
¼   teaspoon vanilla extract
3   ice cubes

Combine all ingredients except ice in a blender; process until smooth. Add ice; process until smooth. Serve immediately. **Yield:** 2 (1-cup) servings.

Per Serving:

Calories 115	**Fiber** 0.5g
Fat 0.4g (sat 0.2g)	**Cholesterol** 2mg
Protein 5.9g	**Sodium** 112mg
Carbohydrate 22.0g	**Exchanges** 1 Starch, ½ Skim Milk

Prep: 20 minutes

Chocolate-Peppermint Parfaits

⅓ cup finely crushed sugar-free hard peppermint candies
     (about 11 candies), divided
2¼ cups frozen fat-free whipped topping, thawed
1   (1.4-ounce) package sugar-free instant chocolate pudding mix
1¾ cups fat-free milk

Set aside 1 tablespoon crushed candies. Fold remaining crushed candies into whipped topping; set aside ½ cup plus 2 tablespoons topping mixture. Spoon half of remaining whipped topping mixture evenly into 5 parfait glasses.

Prepare pudding mix according to package directions, using fat-free milk. Layer half of pudding evenly over topping mixture in glasses. Repeat layers.

Top each parfait with 2 tablespoons reserved topping mixture; sprinkle evenly with reserved tablespoon crushed candies. **Yield:** 5 servings.

Test Kitchen Secret: To crush the peppermints, place the candies in a heavy-duty zip-top plastic bag. Seal the bag, and crush the candy by pounding it with a meat mallet or a heavy rolling pin.

Per Serving:

Calories 132	Fiber 0.0g
Fat 0.2g (sat 0.1g)	Cholesterol 2mg
Protein 3.4g	Sodium 262mg
Carbohydrate 30.5g	Exchanges 2 Starch

Prep: 11 minutes   Freeze: 40 minutes   Stand: 1 hour

Butter Pecan Ice Cream

Go Nuts:

Pecans contain monounsaturated fat—a good-for-you kind of fat that can help reduce the risk of heart disease. Nuts also provide other beneficial nutrients, including vitamin E, protein, and some fiber. Evidence continues to show that the monounsaturated fat in nuts can decrease blood cholesterol levels.

2   tablespoons light butter, melted
½   cup finely chopped pecans, toasted
1½   cups 2% reduced-fat milk
1   cup fat-free half-and-half
½   cup egg substitute
½   cup "measures-like-sugar" calorie-free sweetener
¼   cup "measures-like-sugar" brown sugar calorie-free sweetener
1   teaspoon vanilla extract
⅛   teaspoon salt

Melt butter in a small skillet over medium-high heat. Add pecans, and cook, stirring frequently, 9 minutes or until pecans are toasted.

Combine nuts and remaining ingredients. Pour mixture into freezer container of a 2-quart hand-turned or electric freezer. Freeze according to manufacturer's instructions.

Pack freezer with additional ice and rock salt, and let stand 1 hour before serving. **Yield:** 8 (½-cup) servings.

Per Serving:

Calories 137
Fat 8.0g (sat 1.9g)
Protein 3.8g
Carbohydrate 18.2g
Fiber 0.7g
Cholesterol 7mg
Sodium 131mg
Exchanges 1 Starch, 1½ Fat

Prep: 8 minutes   Cook: 10 minutes per batch

Chocolate Chip Cookies

2⅓ cups all-purpose flour
½   teaspoon baking soda
¾   cup packed brown sugar
¾   cup stick margarine, softened
¾   cup "measures-like-sugar" calorie-free sweetener
½   cup egg substitute
2   teaspoons vanilla extract
1¼ cups semisweet chocolate minichips

Lightly spoon flour into dry measuring cups; level with a knife. Combine flour and baking soda in a large bowl; set aside.
Preheat oven to 350°.
Beat brown sugar, margarine, and sweetener with a mixer at medium speed until blended. Add egg substitute and vanilla, beating well. Gradually add dry ingredients, beating well. Stir in chocolate minichips.
Drop dough by rounded tablespoonfuls onto ungreased baking sheets. Bake at 350° for 10 minutes or until golden. Remove cookies from baking sheets, and cool completely on wire racks. **Yield:** 4 dozen cookies.

Per Cookie:

Calories 88	Fiber 0.2g
Fat 3.9g (sat 1.2g)	Cholesterol 0mg
Protein 0.9g	Sodium 47mg
Carbohydrate 13.8g	Exchanges 1 Starch, ½ Fat

(Photograph on page 54 with Oatmeal-Raisin Cookies)

Nutrition Note:
New guidelines from the American Diabetes Association say that you don't have to omit all sugar from your diet when you have diabetes. But you do need to monitor the total amount of carbohydrate you eat each day.

Prep: 12 minutes   Chill: 1 hour   Cook: 7 minutes per batch

Oatmeal-Raisin Cookies

¼   cup egg substitute
½   cup raisins
¾   cup "measures-like-sugar" calorie-free sweetener
¼   cup packed brown sugar
⅓   cup margarine, softened
⅓   cup apple butter
½   teaspoon ground cinnamon
½   teaspoon vanilla extract
1   cup all-purpose flour
1½   cups quick-cooking oats
½   teaspoon baking soda
Cooking spray

Test Kitchen Secret:
Soaking the raisins
in egg substitute
moistens and
plumps the raisins.
Plus, it keeps the
flour from sticking
to the raisins, so the
cookies come out of
the oven moist and
chewy. Remember to
store cookies in an
airtight container.

Combine egg substitute and raisins in a small bowl. Cover and chill 1 hour.

Preheat oven to 375°.

Beat sweetener, brown sugar, and margarine in a large bowl with a mixer at medium speed until blended. Add apple butter, cinnamon, and vanilla; beat well. Lightly spoon flour into a dry measuring cup; level with a knife. Stir in flour, oats, baking soda, and raisin mixture.

Drop dough by rounded tablespoonfuls onto baking sheets coated with cooking spray. Bake at 375° for 7 to 8 minutes or until lightly browned. Cool 1 minute on baking sheets. Remove cookies from baking sheets; cool completely on wire racks. **Yield:** 3 dozen cookies.

Per Cookie:

Calories 61	Fiber 0.6g
Fat 1.6g (sat 0.4g)	Cholesterol 0mg
Protein 1.1g	Sodium 42mg
Carbohydrate 13.1g	Exchange 1 Starch

Prep: 25 minutes   Cook: 10 minutes

Strawberry Shortcakes

Garnishing Ideas:

Top each shortcake with a dollop of whipped topping or one strawberry slice and a mint sprig. This won't add any calories or carbohydrate and your family will appreciate your effort to make the dessert extra special.

2   cups strawberries, sliced
2   tablespoons "measures-like-sugar" calorie-free sweetener
2   tablespoons low-sugar strawberry spread
1¾ cups all-purpose flour
2   teaspoons baking powder
¼   teaspoon baking soda
¼   teaspoon salt
2   teaspoons "measures-like-sugar" calorie-free sweetener
3   tablespoons reduced-calorie margarine
¾   cup plain fat-free yogurt
Frozen fat-free whipped topping, thawed (optional)
Mint sprigs (optional)

Preheat oven to 425°.

Stir together first 3 ingredients. Set aside.

Spoon flour into dry measuring cups; level with a knife. Combine flour, baking powder, and next 3 ingredients; cut in margarine with a pastry blender or 2 knives until mixture resembles coarse meal. Add yogurt, stirring just until dry ingredients are moist. Turn dough out onto a floured surface; knead 4 times. Roll to a ½-inch thickness; cut into 6 rounds with a 3-inch cutter. Place on an ungreased baking sheet. Bake at 425° for 10 minutes. Remove from baking sheet; cool on a wire rack.

Cut each biscuit in half horizontally. Spoon strawberry mixture evenly over bottom halves of biscuits. Place tops of biscuits on strawberries, cut sides down. Top with whipped topping and mint, if desired. **Yield:** 6 servings.

Per Shortcake:

Calories 212	Fiber 2.3g
Fat 3.4g (sat 0.7g)	Cholesterol 1mg
Protein 5.9g	Sodium 406mg
Carbohydrate 42.7g	Exchanges 1½ Starch, 1 Fruit, 1 Fat

Prep: 15 minutes   Cook: 23 minutes

Raisin-Date Cake

1   cup coarsely chopped dates
1   cup raisins
1   cup water
¼   cup margarine
1   cup all-purpose flour
1   teaspoon baking soda
½   teaspoon cinnamon
½   teaspoon ground nutmeg
¼   teaspoon salt
2   large eggs, lightly beaten
1   teaspoon vanilla extract
½   cup chopped pecans
Cooking spray

Preheat oven to 350°.

Combine first 3 ingredients in a saucepan; bring to a boil over medium heat. Cook, uncovered, 7 minutes or until almost all water is evaporated, stirring occasionally. Remove from heat; stir in margarine. Cool to room temperature.

Lightly spoon flour into a dry measuring cup; level with a knife. Combine flour and next 4 ingredients. Add eggs and vanilla, stirring well. Add fruit mixture to flour mixture, and stir well; fold in pecans.

Pour batter into an 8-inch square baking pan coated with cooking spray. Bake at 350° for 23 minutes or until a wooden pick inserted in center comes out clean. **Yield:** 9 servings (serving size: 1 square).

Per Serving:

Calories 145	**Fiber** 1.8g
Fat 6.0g (sat 1.0g)	**Cholesterol** 27mg
Protein 2.5g	**Sodium** 152mg
Carbohydrate 22.0g	**Exchanges** 1½ Starch, 1 Fat

Prep: 15 minutes   Cook: 1 hour 10 minutes

Vanilla Pound Cake

Butter-flavored cooking spray
1   tablespoon dry breadcrumbs
6   tablespoons butter or margarine, softened
1½   cups sugar
¾   cup egg substitute
1   teaspoon vanilla extract
½   teaspoon almond extract
½   teaspoon baking soda
¾   cup reduced-fat sour cream
2   cups sifted cake flour
¼   teaspoon salt

Preheat oven to 325°.

Coat an 8½ x 4½-inch loaf pan with cooking spray. Dust pan with breadcrumbs. Set aside.

Beat butter with a mixer at medium speed until creamy; add sugar, beating well. Add egg substitute and extracts; beat well. Stir baking soda into sour cream. Combine flour and salt; add to butter mixture alternately with sour cream mixture, beginning and ending with flour mixture. Beat with mixer just until blended after each addition. Pour batter into prepared pan. Bake at 325° for 1 hour and 10 minutes. Cool in pan 10 minutes. Remove from pan; cool completely on a wire rack.

Yield: 16 servings (serving size: 1 slice).

Per Serving:

Calories 183	Fiber 0.4g
Fat 5.7g (sat 1.7g)	Cholesterol 4mg
Protein 2.7g	Sodium 151mg
Carbohydrate 30.4g	Exchanges 2 Starch, 1 Fat

(Photograph on page 2)

***Nutrition Note:** Butter and margarine have the same amount of fat. The fat in butter is mostly saturated, which is not heart healthy. Stick margarine contains trans fat, a type of fat that has also been linked to heart disease. Your best bet is to use what you like, but only in small amounts.*

Prep: 25 minutes   Cook: 1 hour 5 minutes

Chocolate Marbled Pound Cake

¼   cup butter or margarine, softened
3   tablespoons vegetable shortening
1   cup sugar
3   large egg whites
1   cup low-fat buttermilk
½   teaspoon baking soda
2¼ cups sifted cake flour
¼   teaspoon salt
1   teaspoon almond extract
1   teaspoon vanilla extract
2½ tablespoons unsweetened cocoa
3   tablespoons boiling water
2   tablespoons "measures-like-sugar" calorie-free
        sweetener
Baking spray with flour (such as Baker's Joy)

Preheat oven to 325°.

Beat butter and shortening with a mixer at medium speed until creamy. Gradually add sugar, beating at high speed until light and fluffy (about 5 minutes). Add egg whites, one at a time, beating after each addition.

Combine buttermilk and baking soda. Combine flour and salt. Add flour mixture to butter mixture alternately with buttermilk mixture, beating at low speed and beginning and ending with flour mixture. Stir in almond and vanilla extracts. Spoon 2 cups batter into a separate bowl; set aside.

Stir together cocoa and boiling water. Add cocoa mixture and sweetener to remaining batter in bowl. Spoon white batter alternately with chocolate batter into a 9 x 5-inch loaf pan coated with baking spray. Swirl batters gently with a knife. Bake at 325° for 1 hour and 5 minutes or until a wooden pick inserted in center

comes out clean. Cool in pan 10 minutes on a wire rack; remove from pan, and cool completely on wire rack. **Yield:** 16 servings (serving size: 1 slice).

Per Serving:

Calories 159	**Fiber** 0.5g
Fat 5.3g (sat 1.3g)	**Cholesterol** 1mg
Protein 2.5g	**Sodium** 131mg
Carbohydrate 26.7g	**Exchanges** 2 Starch, 1 Fat

Chocolate-Peanut Butter Bread Pudding

Truth About
Chocolate:
Research has shown
that chocolate and
cocoa contain
some of the same
antioxidants found
in fruit, vegetables,
tea, and red wine.
But it's still not
known just what
chocolate's
antioxidants do
in the body. There
are a multitude of
studies showing a
link between fruits
and vegetables and
a decreased risk of
cancer, but no
direct studies show
the same link for
chocolate.

4   (1-ounce) slices reduced-calorie white bread, cut into 1-inch cubes
¼   cup semisweet chocolate minichips
1   cup fat-free milk
¼   cup "measures-like-sugar" brown sugar calorie-free sweetener
¼   cup egg substitute
¼   cup creamy peanut butter
Cooking spray

Preheat oven to 350°.

Place bread cubes in a large bowl; sprinkle with chocolate minichips.

Combine milk and next 3 ingredients in container of a blender; process until smooth. Pour milk mixture over bread mixture; stir to coat. Let stand 10 minutes.

Transfer mixture to a 1-quart baking dish coated with cooking spray. Bake at 350° for 30 minutes or until pudding is firm. Serve immediately. **Yield:** 4 (¾-cup) servings.

Per Serving:

Calories 246	Fiber 3.6g
Fat 12.6g (sat 3.5g)	Cholesterol 1mg
Protein 10.5g	Sodium 270mg
Carbohydrate 26.8g	Exchanges 2 Starch, 1 Medium-Fat Meat, 1 Fat

Prep: 18 minutes   Cook: 45 minutes

Blackberry Cobbler

6   cups fresh blackberries
½   cup "measures-like-sugar" calorie-free sweetener
2   tablespoons orange juice
1   cup all-purpose flour
1¼   teaspoons baking powder
¼   teaspoon baking soda
¼   teaspoon salt
⅓   cup "measures-like-sugar" calorie-free sweetener
⅓   cup vanilla low-fat yogurt
⅓   cup fat-free milk
3   tablespoons reduced-calorie margarine, softened
1   tablespoon "measures-like-sugar" calorie-free sweetener

Cobbler Topper:
If you're not over your carbohydrate allowance for the meal, top the warm cobbler with a small scoop of no-sugar-added ice cream. A ½-cup serving of ice cream usually has about 15 to 18 grams of carbohydrate.

Preheat oven to 350°.

Combine first 3 ingredients; toss lightly. Spoon into an 11 x 7-inch baking dish.

Lightly spoon flour into a dry measuring cup; level with a knife. Combine flour and next 4 ingredients in a medium bowl. Add yogurt, milk, and margarine; beat with a mixer at medium speed until smooth. Dollop over blackberry mixture.

Bake at 350° for 20 minutes. Sprinkle 1 tablespoon sweetener evenly over cobbler. Bake an additional 25 minutes or until golden. Serve warm. **Yield:** 10 (½-cup) servings.

Per Serving:

Calories 147	Fiber 4.9g
Fat 2.2g (sat 0.4g)	Cholesterol 1mg
Protein 2.6g	Sodium 202mg
Carbohydrate 39.7g	Exchanges 1 Starch, 1½ Fruit

Prep: 30 minutes   Cook: 40 minutes

Homestyle Apple Pie

1	(5.5-ounce) can apple juice
5	medium Granny Smith apples, peeled, cored, and thinly sliced
1	teaspoon ground cinnamon
½	teaspoon ground nutmeg
⅓	cup water
1	tablespoon cornstarch
1	(15-ounce) package refrigerated piecrust dough
3	tablespoons margarine

Apple Advice:
We tested this recipe using Granny Smith apples, known for their crisp, tart texture and flavor. You can substitute other varieties such as Braeburn, Baldwin, Cortland, Rome Beauty, Winesap, and York Imperial.

Preheat oven to 450°.

Combine first 4 ingredients in a large saucepan. Cook over medium-high heat 7 minutes or until apple juice is slightly reduced. Combine water and cornstarch, stirring until smooth; stir into apple mixture. Cook, stirring constantly, until thick. Remove from heat, and set aside.

Unfold 1 piecrust, and press out fold lines. Roll into a 9½-inch circle. Place piecrust in pie plate. Spoon in filling; dot with margarine.

Unfold remaining piecrust, roll into a 9½-inch circle, and place over filling. Fold edges under, and flute. Cut slits in top to allow steam to escape. Bake at 450° for 10 minutes; reduce heat to 350°, and bake 30 minutes or until lightly browned. **Yield:** 10 servings (serving size: 1 slice).

Per Serving:

Calories 265	Fiber 1.4g
Fat 14.3g (sat 5.4g)	Cholesterol 8mg
Protein 1.7g	Sodium 191mg
Carbohydrate 32.9g	Exchanges 1 Starch, 1 Fruit, 3 Fat

Prep: 10 minutes   Cook: 50 minutes

Cherry Pie

Sugar Substitutes:
Read the package
label to see which
sweeteners are more
suitable for baking.
For cakes and pies,
we test our recipes
with Splenda.

3   (14.5-ounce) cans pitted tart cherries packed in water, drained
2½   tablespoons quick-cooking tapioca
¾   cup "measures-like-sugar" calorie-free sweetener
1   teaspoon almond extract
1   (15-ounce) package refrigerated piecrust dough
1   tablespoon light butter

Preheat oven to 425°.

Combine first 4 ingredients, stirring well. Set aside.

Unfold piecrusts. Fit 1 piecrust into a 9-inch pie plate according to package directions. Spoon cherry mixture into crust; dot with butter.

Roll remaining piecrust to press out fold line; transfer to top of pie. Fold edges under, and crimp. Cut slits in top of pastry to allow steam to escape.

Bake at 425° for 10 minutes; reduce oven temperature to 375°, and bake an additional 40 minutes, shielding pie with aluminum foil to prevent excessive browning, if necessary. **Yield:** 10 servings (serving size: 1 slice).

Per Serving:

Calories 256	Fiber 0.9g
Fat 11.7g (sat 5.1g)	Cholesterol 10mg
Protein 2.3g	Sodium 170mg
Carbohydrate 43.5g	Exchanges 1 Starch, 1½ Fruit, 2 Fat

FISH & SHELLFISH

Herb-Crusted Salmon, page 71

Oven-Fried Catfish • Grilled Trout • Crispy Orange Roughy

Herb-Crusted Salmon • Crab Cakes

Cajun Oven-Fried Oysters with Spicy Cocktail Sauce

Shrimp-Sausage Jambalaya • Shrimp Scampi

Oven-Fried Catfish

Test Kitchen Secret:
Cornflakes and a
coating of cooking
spray create a
mighty crunch for
the catfish fillets.

¾   cup crushed cornflakes
¾   teaspoon celery salt
¼   teaspoon onion powder
¼   teaspoon paprika
Dash of pepper
4   (6-ounce) skinless farm-raised catfish fillets
Cooking spray

Preheat oven to 350°.

Combine first 5 ingredients; set aside. Cut fillets in half. Spray with cooking spray; coat with cornflake mixture. Arrange in a single layer on a baking sheet coated with cooking spray. Spray fish with cooking spray.

Bake, uncovered, at 350° for 30 minutes or until fish flakes easily when tested with a fork. **Yield:** 4 servings.

Per Serving:

Calories 247	Fiber 0.2g
Fat 8.7g (sat 1.6g)	Cholesterol 77mg
Protein 25.5g	Sodium 673mg
Carbohydrate 14.0g	Exchanges 1 Starch, 3 Lean Meat

Fish Market

If you can't find catfish, any type of white fish fillets will do. Here are some good choices for this recipe. Note: 6 ounces raw fish equals 4 ounces cooked.

Fish (4 ounces cooked)	Total Fat	Saturated Fat
Flounder	2.0 grams	0.7 grams
Haddock	1.4 grams	0.0 grams
Orange Roughy	1.4 grams	0.0 grams
Pollock	1.4 grams	0.0 grams

Prep: 5 minutes   Marinate: 2 hours   Cook: 8 minutes

Grilled Trout

3   (6-ounce) whole trout fillets
2   tablespoons olive oil
1/4   teaspoon grated lemon rind
1   tablespoon fresh lemon juice
3/4   teaspoon dried oregano
1/2   teaspoon paprika
1/2   teaspoon salt
1/4   teaspoon pepper
Cooking spray

Place trout in a shallow dish. Combine olive oil and next 6 ingredients; pour over trout. Cover and marinate in refrigerator 2 hours.

Prepare grill.

Remove trout from marinade, reserving marinade. Place marinade in a small saucepan; cook over medium heat 3 minutes.

Place trout fillets, skin sides up, in a grill basket coated with cooking spray. Brush with cooked marinade. Cover and grill 4 minutes on each side or until fish flakes easily when tested with a fork. **Yield:** 3 servings.

Per Serving:

Calories 281	**Fiber** 0.3g
Fat 16.7g (sat 3.4g)	**Cholesterol** 91mg
Protein 30.3g	**Sodium** 465mg
Carbohydrate 1.0g	**Exchanges** 4 Medium-Fat Meat

Go Fish:

Trout is considered a freshwater "fat" fish because it has an oil content of more than 5 percent. (But the fat in fish is heart-healthy fat.) Fat fish have a stronger flavor than lean fish, and the color is darker because of the oil distributed in the flesh. Fat fish are especially suitable for grilling and smoking. Other fat fish include amberjack, catfish, mackerel, mullet, pompano, salmon, sardines, tuna, and whitefish.

Prep: 5 minutes   Cook: 8 minutes

Crispy Orange Roughy

Test Kitchen Secret:
Sprinkle fillets
with flour, dip in
an egg white wash,
and then coat with
seasoned cornmeal
for a surprisingly
crispy crust.

2   large egg whites, lightly beaten
2   tablespoons water
¼   cup cornmeal
¼   cup grated Parmesan cheese
½   teaspoon dried oregano
½   teaspoon dried parsley flakes
¼   teaspoon salt
¼   teaspoon pepper
6   (6-ounce) orange roughy fillets
3   tablespoons all-purpose flour
Cooking spray
1   tablespoon vegetable oil

Combine egg whites and water in a shallow dish. Combine cornmeal and next 5 ingredients in a medium bowl; stir well.

Sprinkle each side of fillets with flour. Dip fillets into egg white mixture, and dredge in cornmeal mixture.

Coat a large nonstick skillet with cooking spray; add oil. Place skillet over medium-high heat until hot. Add fillets; cook 4 to 5 minutes on each side or until fish flakes easily when tested with a fork. **Yield:** 6 servings.

Per Serving:

Calories 187

Fat 4.7g (sat 1.0g)

Protein 28.4g

Carbohydrate 5.8g

Fiber 0.2g

Cholesterol 37mg

Sodium 300mg

Exchanges ½ Starch, 4 Very Lean Meat

Herb-Crusted Salmon

¼ cup chopped fresh parsley
2 tablespoons chopped fresh rosemary
2 tablespoons chopped fresh tarragon
2 tablespoons chopped fresh oregano
2 (6-ounce) skinless salmon fillets
1 tablespoon olive oil
2 garlic cloves, minced

Preheat oven to 350°.

Combine first 4 ingredients in a shallow dish. Dredge one side of each fillet in herb mixture.

Heat oil in a medium ovenproof skillet over medium heat; add garlic and sauté until tender. Add fish, coated side down, and cook 5 minutes or until browned on coated side.

Turn salmon, and place, uncovered, in oven. Bake at 350° for 7 minutes or until fish flakes with a fork. **Yield:** 2 servings.

Note: A cast iron skillet works great for this recipe. If you don't have one, you can ovenproof a skillet by wrapping the handle tightly with aluminum foil.

Per Serving:

Calories 273	Fiber 0.6g
Fat 13.0g (sat 1.9g)	Cholesterol 88mg
Protein 34.7g	Sodium 120mg
Carbohydrate 2.8g	Exchanges 5 Lean Meat

(Photograph on page 67)

Nutrition Note: Eating fish twice a week, especially fish such as salmon, is a great way to reduce your risk of heart disease. Salmon is high in omega-3 fat, a type of fat that is good for the heart.

Crab Cakes

Simple Supper:

For an easy meal,
serve these hearty
crab cakes with a
tossed green salad.

1	pound fresh lump crabmeat, drained
¾	cup dry breadcrumbs
¼	cup light mayonnaise
1	tablespoon grated Parmesan cheese
1¼	teaspoons Italian seasoning
1½	teaspoons Worcestershire sauce
⅛	teaspoon salt
⅛	teaspoon freshly ground black pepper
1	large egg, lightly beaten
2	to 3 green onions, thinly sliced (about ⅓ cup)
1	medium jalapeño pepper, seeded and diced

Cooking spray
Lemon wedges (optional)
Cocktail sauce (optional)

Preheat oven to 400°.

Combine first 11 ingredients in a large bowl. Shape into 8 patties, and place on a baking sheet coated with cooking spray.

Bake at 400° for 5 minutes on each side or until golden. Serve with lemon wedges and cocktail sauce, if desired. **Yield:** 4 servings (serving size: 2 crab cakes).

Per Serving:

Calories 270	**Fiber** 0.9g
Fat 9.0g (sat 1.9g)	**Cholesterol** 175mg
Protein 28.0g	**Sodium** 735mg
Carbohydrate 17.6g	**Exchanges** 1 Starch, 3½ Lean Meat

Cajun Oven-Fried Oysters with Spicy Cocktail Sauce

Draining Oysters:

To drain oysters well, place them on paper towels for a few minutes before coating with cornmeal mixture.

½ cup ketchup
1 tablespoon prepared horseradish
1 teaspoon fresh lemon juice
½ teaspoon Worcestershire sauce
½ cup yellow cornmeal
1 teaspoon paprika
½ teaspoon salt
¼ teaspoon ground red pepper
¼ teaspoon black pepper
32 medium oysters, drained well
2 tablespoons vegetable oil
Lemon wedges (optional)

Preheat oven to 450°.

Combine ketchup and next 3 ingredients; set aside.

Combine cornmeal and next 4 ingredients in a bowl; stir well. Transfer to a plate. Add oysters in batches of 8; toss to coat completely.

Coat a jelly roll pan evenly with oil; place in oven and heat 3 minutes or until very hot. Arrange oysters on pan in a single layer. Bake at 450° for 8 minutes; turn and bake an additional 8 minutes or until golden. Remove oysters from pan. Serve immediately with cocktail sauce. Garnish with lemon wedges, if desired. **Yield:** 4 servings (serving size: 8 oysters and 2 tablespoons sauce).

Per Serving:

Calories 219	Fiber 1.8g
Fat 9.4g (sat 1.1g)	Cholesterol 28mg
Protein 7.8g	Sodium 880mg
Carbohydrate 27.5g	Exchanges 2 Starch, 1 Very Lean Meat

Prep: 20 minutes   Cook: 40 minutes

Shrimp-Sausage Jambalaya

Cooking spray
½   pound turkey kielbasa sausage, sliced
1½   tablespoons olive oil
2   cups chopped onion
1½   cups chopped green bell pepper
¾   cup chopped celery
2   garlic cloves, minced
2½   cups fat-free, less-sodium chicken broth
2   tablespoons tomato paste
1   teaspoon hot sauce
1   teaspoon Worcestershire sauce
1   teaspoon salt-free Creole seasoning
¾   cup uncooked long-grain rice
½   pound large shrimp, peeled and deveined
½   cup chopped green onions

Sodium Solution: If you need to reduce the sodium in this recipe, use low-sodium versions of tomato paste and chicken broth, and reduced-sodium Worcestershire sauce. If you use these products, the sodium value will be 660 milligrams per serving.

Coat a Dutch oven with cooking spray; place over medium-high heat until hot. Add sausage; sauté 4 minutes. Drain, and set aside.

Add oil and next 4 ingredients to pan. Sauté 8 minutes or until tender. Add broth and next 4 ingredients. Bring to a boil; add rice. Return to a boil; cover, reduce heat, and simmer *22* minutes or until rice is tender. Add shrimp and reserved sausage; cover and cook 3 minutes. Stir in green onions. Let stand 5 minutes. **Yield:** 4 (1½-cup) servings.

Per Serving:

Calories 350	Fiber 4.2g
Fat 7.5g (sat 1.4g)	Cholesterol 84mg
Protein 20.5g	Sodium 1,023mg
Carbohydrate 49.3g	Exchanges 2½ Starch, 2 Vegetable, 1 Lean Meat, 1 Fat

Shrimp Scampi

Shortcut Shrimp:
To save time, buy
shrimp that already
have been peeled
and deveined. For
this recipe, you'll
need to buy about
1⅛ pounds peeled
and deveined raw
shrimp.

8	ounces uncooked angel hair pasta
¼	cup reduced-calorie margarine
1½	pounds medium shrimp, peeled and deveined
4	garlic cloves, minced
½	cup dry white wine
¼	teaspoon salt
¼	teaspoon freshly ground black pepper
½	cup grated Romano cheese
1	tablespoon chopped fresh parsley

Cook pasta according to package directions, omitting salt and fat; drain pasta, and keep warm.

Melt margarine in a large nonstick skillet over medium heat. Add shrimp and garlic, and sauté 3 to 5 minutes or until shrimp are done; add wine, salt, and pepper. Bring to a boil, and cook 30 seconds, stirring constantly.

Place pasta on a large serving platter. Pour shrimp mixture over pasta; sprinkle with cheese and parsley, and toss gently. Serve immediately.

Yield: 4 servings (serving size: about 4 ounces cooked shrimp and 1 cup pasta).

Per Serving:

Calories 389	**Fiber** 1.1g
Fat 11.3g (sat 3.6g)	**Cholesterol** 225mg
Protein 37.4g	**Sodium** 907mg
Carbohydrate 33.5g	**Exchanges** 2 Starch, 4 Lean Meat

MEATS

Favorite Pot Roast, page 84

Barbecue Meat Loaf • Salisbury Steak with Gravy • Stuffed Peppers
Shepherd's Pie • Beef Stroganoff • Favorite Pot Roast
Braised Lamb with Beans • Veal Parmigiana
Country-Style Pork Chops • Apricot-Glazed Ham Steaks

Barbecue Meat Loaf

Homestyle Meal:
Serve this saucy
meat loaf with
mashed potatoes
and steamed
carrots. You can
prepare low-fat
mashed potatoes
with one-half of a
22-ounce package
of frozen mashed
potatoes, cooking
according to
package directions.
Use 1⅓ cups
fat-free milk,
2 tablespoons light
butter, and ¼
teaspoon each of
salt and pepper.

1	pound ground round
½	cup barbecue sauce, divided
¼	cup chopped onion
¼	cup Italian-seasoned breadcrumbs
2	large egg whites
¼	teaspoon pepper

Preheat oven to 375°.

Combine meat, ¼ cup barbecue sauce, onion, breadcrumbs, egg whites, and pepper in a large bowl; stir well.

Shape mixture into a 7 x 5-inch loaf on a rack in a roasting pan. Spread remaining ¼ cup barbecue sauce over loaf. Bake at 375° for 25 to 28 minutes or to desired degree of doneness. **Yield:** 4 servings (serving size: 1 slice).

Per Serving:

Calories 228	Fiber 0.5g
Fat 7.6g (sat 2.6g)	Cholesterol 70mg
Protein 27.7g	Sodium 535mg
Carbohydrate 10.4g	Exchanges 1 Starch, 3 Lean Meat

Salisbury Steak with Gravy

Room for Mushrooms:

If you're buying loose mushrooms, choose those that are firm and unblemished. They should have an earthy, fresh smell and a firm, moist flesh.

Whether you buy them loose or pre-packaged, keep mushrooms in a cool, dry place. Refrigerating them in either plastic or paper containers will help keep them fresh.

To clean mushrooms, give them a quick rinse and pat dry with paper towels or wipe them off with a paper towel.

1½	pounds ground round
1¾	cups soft breadcrumbs (about 4 slices bread)
½	cup chopped onion
¼	cup chopped green bell pepper
2	tablespoons steak sauce
1	large egg white
½	teaspoon salt
¾	teaspoon black pepper, divided
2	teaspoons reduced-calorie margarine
2	cups sliced mushrooms
1	shallot, finely chopped
2	tablespoons all-purpose flour
¼	cup dry white wine
1	(14.25-ounce) can fat-free, less-sodium beef broth

Preheat broiler.

Combine first 7 ingredients and ½ teaspoon pepper; shape into 6 patties. Place on a rack in broiler pan. Broil 6 minutes on each side.

Melt margarine in a nonstick skillet over medium-high heat. Add mushrooms and shallot; sauté 3 minutes. Add flour, and cook 1 minute, stirring constantly. Add wine; reduce heat, and simmer, uncovered, 2 minutes. Add broth and remaining ¼ teaspoon pepper; simmer, uncovered, 7 minutes or until reduced by one-fourth, stirring occasionally. Spoon gravy over patties. **Yield:** 6 servings (serving size: 1 patty and ¼ cup gravy).

Per Serving:

Calories 251	Fiber 1.2g
Fat 7.3g (sat 2.3g)	Cholesterol 66mg
Protein 29.8g	Sodium 499mg
Carbohydrate 15.3g	Exchanges 1 Starch, 3½ Lean Meat

Prep: 17 minutes   Cook: 20 minutes

Stuffed Peppers

6	green bell peppers (about 2 pounds)
¾	pound ground round
1¾	cups finely chopped onion (about 1 large)
1	garlic clove, minced
1	(29-ounce) can tomato sauce
1½	cups cooked rice
1	teaspoon dried marjoram
1	teaspoon dried oregano
¼	teaspoon pepper
⅛	teaspoon salt
6	tablespoons fat-free sour cream

Timesaving Tip:
Use boil-in-bag rice to get cooked rice in 10 minutes. You can cook the rice while the meat is simmering. One regular-size bag (about 3½ ounces) yields 2 cups cooked rice.

Preheat oven to 350°.

Cut tops off bell peppers. Remove and discard seeds and membranes. Finely chop pepper tops, discarding stems; set chopped pepper aside. Cook pepper cups in boiling water to cover 5 minutes. Drain peppers; set aside.

Cook chopped green bell pepper, beef, onion, and garlic in a Dutch oven over medium-high heat 5 minutes or until beef is browned, stirring to crumble. Add tomato sauce and next 5 ingredients. Bring to a boil; reduce heat and simmer, uncovered, 6 minutes, stirring often.

Spoon beef mixture evenly into pepper cups; place in an 11 x 7-inch baking dish. Add hot water to dish to depth of ½ inch. Bake, uncovered, at 350° for 20 to 25 minutes or until thoroughly heated. Spoon 1 tablespoon sour cream on each pepper before serving. **Yield:** 6 servings.

Per Serving:

Calories 234	Fiber 5.6g
Fat 3.9g (sat 1.2g)	Cholesterol 33mg
Protein 18.0g	Sodium 962mg
Carbohydrate 33.6g	Exchanges 1½ Starch, 2 Vegetable, 1 Lean Meat

Shepherd's Pie

Nutrition Note:
A tablespoon of
yogurt-based spread
such as Brummel &
Brown has less than
half the fat of a
tablespoon of
margarine or
butter. You can
substitute light
butter or reduced-
calorie margarine
if you don't have
the spread.

2½ pounds baking potatoes, peeled and cut into eighths
1½ cups fat-free milk, divided
¼ cup egg substitute
2 tablespoons yogurt-based spread
1 teaspoon salt, divided
1 teaspoon pepper, divided
Cooking spray
1½ cups finely chopped onion
2 garlic cloves, minced
1 pound ground round
1 teaspoon dried sage
½ teaspoon ground thyme
¼ cup all-purpose flour
1 (15¼-ounce) can white corn, drained

Place potato in a saucepan; add water to cover. Bring to a boil. Cover, reduce heat, and simmer 15 minutes; drain. Combine potato, ½ cup milk, egg substitute, spread, ½ teaspoon salt, and ½ teaspoon pepper. Beat with mixer 1 minute or until fluffy.

Preheat oven to 350°.

Heat a nonstick skillet coated with cooking spray over medium-high heat. Add onion and garlic; sauté 3 minutes. Add beef, sage, thyme, and ½ teaspoon each salt and pepper. Cook 5 minutes until meat is browned. Combine 1 cup milk and flour; add to beef. Simmer, uncovered, 10 minutes. Pour into an 11 x 7-inch baking dish. Sprinkle with corn, and top with potatoes. Bake, uncovered, at 350° for 30 minutes. **Yield:** 6 (1-cup) servings.

Per Serving:

Calories 387	Fiber 4.2g
Fat 6.2g (sat 1.9g)	Cholesterol 45mg
Protein 25.3g	Sodium 666mg
Carbohydrate 59.0g	Exchanges 4 Starch, 2 Lean Meat

Prep: 18 minutes   Cook: 19 minutes

Beef Stroganoff

Cooking spray
1   pound lean boneless top sirloin steak, cut into ½-inch cubes
½   cup chopped onion
1   cup coarsely chopped mushrooms
1   tablespoon all-purpose flour
½   cup dry white wine
1   cup beef broth
½   teaspoon dried thyme
¼   teaspoon salt
¼   teaspoon pepper
½   cup low-fat sour cream
4   cups hot cooked egg noodles

Place a large nonstick skillet coated with cooking spray over medium-high heat until hot. Add steak and onion, and cook 3 to 5 minutes or until steak is browned, stirring constantly.

Add mushrooms; cook 2 minutes, stirring often. Add flour; cook, stirring constantly, 1 minute. Stir in wine, and simmer 2 minutes. Add broth and next 3 ingredients; simmer, uncovered, 7 to 10 minutes or until reduced by half.

Remove skillet from heat; stir in sour cream. To serve, spoon beef mixture evenly over noodles. **Yield:** 4 servings (serving size: 1 cup noodles and ½ cup meat mixture).

Test Kitchen Secret:
Be sure to use either low-fat or reduced-fat sour cream in the recipe, not fat-free. Fat-free sour cream contains extra water to replace some of the fat, so your sauce won't be very creamy with the fat-free version.

Per Serving:

Calories 438	Fiber 4.2g
Fat 9.9g (sat 3.6g)	Cholesterol 127mg
Protein 36.1g	Sodium 555mg
Carbohydrate 47.8g	Exchanges 3 Starch, 4 Lean Meat

Favorite Pot Roast

Nutrition Note:

Red meat is not off-limits when you're trying to eat healthfully. Lean cuts of beef (chuck roast, eye of round, top round steak, top round roast, sirloin steak, tenderloin steak) are good sources of important nutrients such as protein, B vitamins, iron, and zinc.

¼	cup all-purpose flour
½	teaspoon salt
½	teaspoon pepper
1	(3-pound) boneless chuck roast
2	tablespoons vegetable oil
1	large onion, thinly sliced
1	(10½-ounce) can beef consommé
½	cup water
½	teaspoon dried oregano
¼	teaspoon salt
¼	teaspoon garlic powder
¼	teaspoon pepper
1	bay leaf
6	small round red potatoes, peeled
6	carrots, scraped and cut into 2-inch pieces
3	celery stalks, cut into 2-inch pieces

Combine first 3 ingredients; dredge roast in flour mixture. Heat oil in a Dutch oven over medium-high heat. Add roast; cook until browned on all sides, turning occasionally. Drain. Top with onion and next 7 ingredients. Bring to a boil; cover, reduce heat, and simmer 2½ hours. **Add** potato, carrot, and celery; cover and simmer 30 minutes or until vegetables are tender. Remove and discard bay leaf. **Yield:** 12 servings (serving size: about 3 ounces roast, ¼ cup sauce, and ¼ cup vegetables).

Per Serving:

Calories 230	Fiber 2.0g
Fat 7.7g (sat 2.4g)	Cholesterol 79mg
Protein 27.8g	Sodium 388mg
Carbohydrate 10.9g	Exchanges 1 Starch, 3 Lean Meat

(Photograph on page 77)

Prep: 10 minutes   Cook: 2 hours 45 minutes

Braised Lamb with Beans

2½ pounds lamb shanks
Cooking spray
1   medium onion, chopped (about 1 cup)
1   medium carrot, chopped (about ¾ cup)
½   cup dry white wine
2   cups dried cannellini beans, sorted, washed, and drained
6   cups water
3   thyme sprigs
1   tablespoon chopped fresh rosemary
1   teaspoon salt
½   teaspoon pepper
3   garlic cloves, minced
3   tablespoons fresh lemon juice

Cooking with Spirit:
All of the alcohol from the wine evaporates during cooking, leaving only the flavor behind. You can use chicken broth if you prefer not to use alcohol.

Preheat oven to 350°.
Place an ovenproof Dutch oven over medium heat until hot. Coat lamb with cooking spray; add to pan, and cook 12 minutes or until browned on all sides. Remove lamb from pan. Add onion and carrot to pan; sauté 5 minutes. Add wine; bring to a boil. Reduce heat, and simmer, uncovered, 2 minutes. Add lamb, beans, water, and thyme. Bring to a boil. Transfer to oven, and bake, covered, at 350° for 2 hours. Stir in rosemary and next 3 ingredients. Cover and bake 30 minutes.
Remove meat from bones, and return meat to pan; stir in lemon juice. Cook over medium-high heat until slightly thick. **Yield:** 7 (1-cup) servings.

Per Serving:

Calories 340	Fiber 7.3g
Fat 7.2g (sat 2.5g)	Cholesterol 44mg
Protein 26.9g	Sodium 390mg
Carbohydrate 42.8g	Exchanges 3 Starch, 2½ Lean Meat

(Photograph on page 1)

Prep: 15 minutes   Cook: 18 minutes

Veal Parmigiana

1   (14.5-ounce) can diced tomatoes, undrained
¼   cup dry red wine
1   tablespoon minced fresh basil
1   tablespoon minced fresh thyme
½   cup Italian-seasoned breadcrumbs
1   tablespoon water
1   large egg white
1   pound very thin veal cutlets (¼ inch thick)
Cooking spray
1   tablespoon vegetable oil, divided
¼   cup (1 ounce) shredded part-skim mozzarella cheese

Nutrition Note: Canned tomato products are especially good sources of lycopene, a substance in food that appears to help reduce the risk of prostate cancer. It's also found in fresh tomatoes.

Combine first 4 ingredients in a saucepan; bring to a boil. Reduce heat, and simmer, uncovered, 3 minutes or until slightly thick.

Place breadcrumbs in a shallow dish. Combine water and egg white; beat lightly. Dip veal into egg white mixture, turning to coat; dredge in breadcrumbs.

Coat a large nonstick skillet with cooking spray; add 1½ teaspoons oil. Place over medium-high heat until hot. Add half of veal to pan; cook 1 to 2 minutes on each side or until lightly browned. Remove veal from pan, and keep warm. Recoat skillet with cooking spray, and add remaining 1½ teaspoons oil. Repeat procedure with remaining veal.

Return all veal to pan; pour tomato mixture over veal. Sprinkle cheese over tomato mixture. Cover and cook 3 minutes or until cheese melts.

Yield: 4 servings (serving size: about 3 ounces veal plus sauce).

Per Serving:

Calories 260	Fiber 2.0g
Fat 8.5g (sat 2.5g)	Cholesterol 98mg
Protein 28.6g	Sodium 761mg
Carbohydrate 16.4g	Exchanges 1 Starch, 3½ Lean Meat

Country-Style Pork Chops

Choose Pork:

*The leanest cuts of
pork are the cuts
with "loin" or "leg"
in the name. Some
lean cuts of pork
include tenderloin,
center loin chop,
top loin chop, and
sirloin roast.*

6   tablespoons all-purpose flour, divided
2   tablespoons dry breadcrumbs
½   teaspoon paprika
¼   teaspoon ground sage
½   teaspoon salt, divided
½   teaspoon garlic pepper, divided
4   (6-ounce) lean center-cut pork loin chops (½ inch thick)
¼   cup egg substitute
2   teaspoons vegetable oil
Cooking spray
½   cup fat-free, less-sodium chicken broth
¾   cup fat-free milk, divided

Combine 2 tablespoons flour, breadcrumbs, paprika, sage, ¼ teaspoon salt, and ¼ teaspoon garlic pepper in a heavy-duty zip-top plastic bag. Dip chops into egg substitute; place in bag with flour. Seal bag; shake until chops are coated. Heat oil in a nonstick skillet coated with cooking spray; add chops. Cook 2 minutes on each side. Add broth; bring to a boil. Cover, reduce heat, and simmer 15 minutes or until tender. Remove chops from pan, reserving liquid in pan, and keep warm.

Combine remaining ¼ cup flour and ¼ cup milk, stirring until smooth; stir flour mixture into liquid in pan with a whisk. Stir in ½ cup milk, ¼ teaspoon salt, and ¼ teaspoon pepper; bring just to a simmer. Cook until thick, stirring constantly; spoon sauce over chops. **Yield:** 4 servings.

Per Serving:

Calories 275	Fiber 0.5g
Fat 10.3g (sat 3.2g)	Cholesterol 68mg
Protein 28.3g	Sodium 564mg
Carbohydrate 14.7g	Exchanges 1 Starch, 3½ Lean Meat

Prep: 3 minutes   Cook: 11 minutes

Apricot-Glazed Ham Steaks

Ham It Up:
Although lean ham
is low in fat, it's
still a high-sodium
meat. If you are on
a low-sodium diet,
you may need to
modify this recipe
by using reduced-
sodium ham.

1   (¾-pound) lean ham
Cooking spray
¼   cup apricot spreadable fruit
¼   cup orange juice
Orange slices (optional)

Slice ham into 4 (3-ounce) slices. Coat a large nonstick skillet with cooking spray; place over medium-high heat until hot. Add ham; cook 2 to 3 minutes on each side or until lightly browned.
Add apricot spread and orange juice to pan, stirring until spread melts. Reduce heat, and simmer 5 to 6 minutes or until ham is glazed. Garnish with orange slices, if desired. **Yield:** 4 servings.

Per Serving:

Calories 127	Fiber 0.0g
Fat 3.6g (sat 1.0g)	Cholesterol 40mg
Protein 15.2g	Sodium 856mg
Carbohydrate 9.1g	Exchanges ½ Fruit, 2 Lean Meat

POULTRY

Easy Barbecued Chicken, page 96

Chicken Pot Pie • Chicken à la King • Chicken and Dumplings
Easy Barbecued Chicken • Baked Buffalo Chicken • Oven-Fried Chicken
Lemon-Herb Roasted Chicken • Thyme-and-Garlic Roasted Turkey Breast
Lattice-Topped Turkey Pie • Red Beans and Rice
Old-Fashioned Turkey Hash

Prep: 11 minutes   Cook: 30 minutes

Chicken Pot Pie

1   (10¾-ounce) can condensed reduced-fat, reduced-sodium
        cream of mushroom soup, undiluted
½   cup fat-free milk
½   teaspoon salt
¼   teaspoon pepper
3   cups chopped cooked chicken breast
2   cups frozen peas and carrots, thawed
½   cup chopped onion
½   cup thinly sliced celery
1   (2-ounce) jar sliced pimiento, drained
1½ cups low-fat baking mix (such as reduced-fat Bisquick)
¾   cup fat-free milk
1   large egg
Fat-free butter spray (such as I Can't Believe It's Not Butter!)
1   tablespoon preshredded fresh Parmesan cheese

Preheat oven to 375°.

Combine soup and next 3 ingredients in a saucepan; bring to a boil. Reduce heat, and simmer, uncovered, 1 minute, stirring constantly until smooth. Stir in chicken, peas and carrots, and next 3 ingredients. Bring to a boil; cover, reduce heat, and simmer 5 minutes. Pour mixture into an 11 x 7-inch baking dish.

Combine baking mix, ¾ cup milk, and egg; stir until smooth. Spread evenly over chicken mixture; coat with butter spray. Sprinkle with cheese. Bake, uncovered, at 375° for 30 to 35 minutes or until golden.

Yield: 6 servings (serving size: about 1⅓ cups).

Personal Pies:

For individual pot pies, pour 1 cup chicken mixture into 6 (8-ounce) ramekins or custard cups, and top each with ¾ cup crust mixture. Spray each with butter spray, and sprinkle with ½ teaspoon Parmesan cheese. Bake, uncovered, at 375° for 30 to 35 minutes or until golden.

Per Serving:

Calories 293	Fiber 2.3g
Fat 5.3g (sat 1.6g)	Cholesterol 85mg
Protein 25.2g	Sodium 883mg
Carbohydrate 35.0g	Exchanges 2 Starch, 1 Vegetable, 2 Lean Meat

Prep: 5 minutes   Cook: 10 minutes

Chicken à la King

Test Kitchen
Secret:
For tender chunks
of cooked chicken,
place 4 (4-ounce)
skinless, boneless
chicken breast
halves on a baking
sheet coated with
cooking spray.
Sprinkle the
chicken with ¼
teaspoon each salt
and pepper. Bake
at 350° for 25
minutes. Cool
slightly and chop.
You'll get about
3 cups chopped
cooked chicken.

1   cup chopped cooked chicken breast
¼   cup fat-free milk
¼   cup frozen green peas, thawed
¼   teaspoon pepper
1   (10¾-ounce) can condensed reduced-fat, reduced-sodium
        cream of chicken soup, undiluted
1   (7-ounce) can sliced mushrooms, drained
1   (2-ounce) jar diced pimiento, drained
2   tablespoons low-fat sour cream
2   slices reduced-calorie whole wheat bread, toasted
Paprika

Combine first 7 ingredients in a large saucepan; cook over low heat 10 minutes, stirring often. Remove from heat. Stir in sour cream.

Cut each slice of toast in half diagonally, and place on serving plates. Spoon 1¼ cups chicken mixture evenly over each serving of toast. Sprinkle with paprika. **Yield:** 2 servings (serving size: 1 slice toast and 1¼ cups chicken mixture).

Per Serving:

Calories 309	Fiber 4.0g
Fat 6.7g (sat 2.6g)	Cholesterol 88mg
Protein 32.2g	Sodium 920mg
Carbohydrate 32.2g	Exchanges 2 Starch, 1 Vegetable, 3 Very Lean Meat

Prep: 12 minutes   Cook: 25 minutes

Chicken and Dumplings

3	(10½-ounce) cans low-sodium chicken broth
1	cup thinly sliced carrot
1	cup thinly sliced celery
½	cup chopped onion
½	teaspoon dried thyme
½	teaspoon dried rosemary, crushed
¼	teaspoon salt
¼	teaspoon pepper
1	pound skinless, boneless chicken breast halves, cut into cubes
1⅓	cups all-purpose flour
1¼	teaspoons baking powder
¼	teaspoon salt
½	cup plus 1 tablespoon fat-free milk
2	tablespoons reduced-calorie margarine, melted

Cubing Chicken:
It's easier to cube raw chicken if you freeze it just until firm to the touch.

Combine first 8 ingredients in a Dutch oven; bring to a boil. Add chicken; cover, reduce heat, and simmer 10 minutes.

Combine flour, baking powder, and ¼ teaspoon salt. Add milk and margarine, stirring to form a stiff dough. Drop dough by heaping table-spoonfuls on top of broth mixture to create 8 dumplings. Cover, reduce heat, and simmer 15 minutes or until dumplings are done. Ladle chicken mixture into 4 bowls; top each serving with dumplings. **Yield:** 4 servings (serving size: 1 cup chicken mixture and 2 dumplings).

Per Serving:

Calories 361	**Fiber** 3.1g
Fat 7.1g (sat 2.0g)	**Cholesterol** 64mg
Protein 31.3g	**Sodium** 698mg
Carbohydrate 42.4g	**Exchanges** 3 Starch, 3 Lean Meat

Easy Barbecued Chicken

½   cup ketchup
2   tablespoons finely chopped onion
2   tablespoons peach or apricot jam
2   tablespoons white vinegar
1   teaspoon Worcestershire sauce
1½   teaspoons chili powder
⅛   teaspoon garlic powder
Cooking spray
4   (6-ounce) skinless chicken breast halves

Prepare grill.

Combine first 7 ingredients in a small saucepan; bring to a boil. Reduce heat, and simmer, uncovered, 5 minutes. Set aside ½ cup sauce; keep warm.

Place chicken, bone side up, on grill rack coated with cooking spray; cover and grill 8 minutes on each side or until done, turning once and basting with remaining barbecue sauce. Serve with reserved ½ cup barbecue sauce. **Yield:** 4 servings (serving size: 1 chicken breast and 2 tablespoons sauce).

Per Serving:

Calories 203	**Fiber** 0.8g
Fat 3.7g (sat 1.0g)	**Cholesterol** 78mg
Protein 29.2g	**Sodium** 451mg
Carbohydrate 16.3g	**Exchanges** 1 Starch, 4 Very Lean Meat

(Photograph on page 91)

Prep: 15 minutes   Cook: 25 minutes

Baked Buffalo Chicken

Cooking spray
1½ teaspoons vegetable oil
4   small chicken thighs (about 1½ pounds), skinned
¼   cup hot sauce
2   tablespoons reduced-calorie margarine, melted
2   tablespoons water
1   tablespoon white vinegar
1   teaspoon celery seeds
⅛   teaspoon pepper
¼   cup reduced-fat blue cheese dressing

Healthy Alternative: These chicken thighs may remind you of the spicy wings served at your local sports grill. But instead of being fried, these are quickly browned in a skillet and baked in a tangy hot sauce mixture.

Preheat oven to 400°.

Coat a nonstick skillet with cooking spray; add oil. Place over medium-high heat until hot. Add chicken; cook 4 minutes on each side. Transfer chicken to an 11 x 7-inch baking dish coated with cooking spray.

Combine hot sauce and next 5 ingredients; pour over chicken. Bake, uncovered, at 400° for 25 minutes. Serve with blue cheese dressing.

Yield: *2 servings (serving size: 2 thighs and 2 tablespoons dressing).*

Per Serving:

Calories 310	Fiber 0.4g
Fat 17.2g (sat 3.8g)	Cholesterol 118mg
Protein 30.1g	Sodium 811mg
Carbohydrate 7.7g	Exchanges ½ Starch, 4 Lean Meat, 1 Fat

Prep: 15 minutes   Soak: 8 hours   Cook: 45 minutes

Oven-Fried Chicken

1 quart water
1 teaspoon salt
6 (4-ounce) chicken drumsticks, skinned
4 (6-ounce) skinless, bone-in chicken breast halves
½ cup low-fat buttermilk
5 cups coarsely crushed cornflakes
2 to 3 teaspoons Creole seasoning
2 teaspoons dried Italian seasoning
½ teaspoon garlic powder
¼ teaspoon freshly ground black pepper
Cooking spray

Perfect Fried Chicken:

This oven-fried chicken doesn't make a greasy mess. Plus, it has plenty of crunch and taste, thanks to cornflakes and Creole and Italian seasonings.

Combine water and salt in a large bowl; add chicken pieces. Cover and chill 8 hours.

Preheat oven to 400°.

Drain chicken; rinse with cold water, and pat dry. Place chicken in a shallow dish; pour buttermilk over chicken, turning pieces to coat.

Combine cornflakes and next 4 ingredients in a large heavy-duty zip-top plastic bag. Place 2 pieces chicken in bag; seal. Shake to coat completely. Remove chicken, and repeat procedure with remaining pieces.

Place coated chicken, bone side down, in a 15 x 10-inch jelly roll pan coated with cooking spray, and spray chicken with cooking spray. Place pan on lowest rack in oven. Bake, uncovered, at 400° for 45 minutes (do not turn). **Yield:** 7 servings (serving size: 2 drumsticks or 1 breast half).

Per Serving:

Calories 262	Fiber 0.6g
Fat 9.6g (sat 2.8g)	Cholesterol 74mg
Protein 24.9g	Sodium 638mg
Carbohydrate 18.4g	Exchanges 1 Starch, 3 Lean Meat

Prep: 16 minutes   Cook: 1 hour   Stand: 15 minutes

Lemon-Herb Roasted Chicken

Homestyle Meal:

Serve this tender
chicken with
steamed vegetables
and hot cooked rice
that has been
tossed with lemon
zest and chopped
fresh herbs.

1	(3-pound) roasting chicken
3	sprigs rosemary, thyme, or sage
2	tablespoons chopped fresh rosemary, thyme, or sage
1	teaspoon grated lemon rind
3	tablespoons fresh lemon juice
¼	teaspoon salt
¼	teaspoon pepper
2	garlic cloves, minced

Preheat oven to 400°.

Remove and discard giblets from chicken. Rinse chicken under cold water; pat dry. Trim excess fat. Starting at neck cavity, loosen skin from breast and drumsticks by inserting fingers, gently pushing between skin and meat.

Place rosemary sprigs under loosened skin over breast. Combine chopped rosemary and remaining 5 ingredients; brush over chicken and in cavity of chicken.

Place chicken on a rack in a roasting pan. Insert meat thermometer into meaty part of thigh, making sure not to touch bone. Bake, uncovered, at 400° for 1 hour or until thermometer registers 180°. Let stand 15 minutes before serving. **Yield:** 6 servings (serving size: about 3 ounces roasted chicken).

Per Serving:

Calories 105	Fiber 0.5g
Fat 2.7g (sat 0.7g)	Cholesterol 57mg
Protein 17.6g	Sodium 161mg
Carbohydrate 1.8g	Exchanges 2½ Very Lean Meat

Prep: 13 minutes   Cook: 1 hour 15 minutes

Thyme-and-Garlic Roasted Turkey Breast

2   teaspoons minced fresh thyme
1   teaspoon grated lemon rind
¼   teaspoon coarsely ground black pepper
⅛   teaspoon salt
2   garlic cloves, crushed
1   (5-pound) turkey breast
Cooking spray
1   lemon, quartered
6   thyme sprigs
Thyme sprigs (optional)

Preheat oven to 400°.

Combine first 5 ingredients in a small bowl. Starting at neck edge, loosen skin from turkey breast by inserting fingers, gently pushing between skin and meat. Rub thyme mixture under loosened skin. Gently press skin to secure.

Place breast, skin side up, on a broiler pan coated with cooking spray. Place lemon quarters and 6 thyme sprigs in cavity. Insert meat thermometer into meaty part of breast, making sure not to touch bone. Bake at 400° for 1 hour and 15 minutes or until thermometer registers 170°. Let stand 10 minutes. Remove skin, and discard. Cut breast into thin slices; garnish with thyme sprigs, if desired. **Yield:** 9 servings (serving size: about 4 ounces).

The Skinny on Turkey:

When you remove the skin from turkey, you remove most of the fat. A 3-ounce portion of turkey breast with skin has about 6 grams of fat; a 3-ounce portion without skin has less than 1 gram of fat.

Per Serving:

Calories 171	Fiber 0.0g
Fat 1.1g (sat 0.3g)	Cholesterol 104mg
Protein 37.6g	Sodium 97mg
Carbohydrate 0.3g	Exchanges 5 Very Lean Meat

Lattice-Topped Turkey Pie

Shortcut Crust:
For an easier
version of our
woven lattice crust,
lay half of the
crescent roll strips
in one direction
across the turkey
mixture. Lay the
remaining strips
perpendicular (at
right angles) to the
first half.

½   cup low-fat mayonnaise
2   tablespoons all-purpose flour
1   cup fat-free milk
1   teaspoon chicken-flavored bouillon granules
1   (10-ounce) package frozen mixed vegetables, thawed and
     drained
2   cups chopped cooked turkey breast
⅛   teaspoon pepper
1   (4-ounce) can reduced-fat refrigerated crescent rolls

Preheat oven to 375°.

Combine mayonnaise and flour in a medium saucepan; stir well with a wire whisk. Stir in milk and bouillon granules. Cook over medium heat, stirring constantly, until mixture is thick and bubbly.

Stir in vegetables, turkey, and pepper; cook until thoroughly heated, stirring occasionally. Spoon mixture into an ungreased 9-inch pie plate.

Unroll crescent rolls, and place rectangular pieces side by side on a lightly floured surface. Press perforations together to seal. Roll dough to a 10-inch square; cut into 1-inch strips. Arrange strips in a lattice design over turkey mixture. Bake at 375° for 15 to 20 minutes or until lightly browned. Let stand 5 minutes. **Yield:** 4 servings (serving size: ¼ of pie).

Per Serving:

Calories 338	**Fiber** 3.0g
Fat 7.7g (sat 1.4g)	**Cholesterol** 65mg
Protein 30.1g	**Sodium** 848mg
Carbohydrate 36.0g	**Exchanges** 2 Starch, 1 Vegetable, 3 Lean Meat

Prep: 10 minutes   Cook: 20 minutes

Red Beans and Rice

1   turkey bacon slice, diced
1   large onion, minced
4   garlic cloves, minced
1   (16-ounce) can red kidney beans, rinsed and drained
1   (14.5-ounce) can no-salt-added stewed tomatoes, undrained
4   ounces low-fat smoked turkey sausage, cut into bite-size pieces
1   teaspoon hot sauce
½   teaspoon freshly ground black pepper
2   bay leaves
1   family-size bag quick-cooking boil-in-bag rice, uncooked

Nutrition Note: *Smoked turkey sausage has about 66 percent less fat than smoked beef and pork sausage. The sodium, however, is about the same.*

Cook bacon in a 3-quart saucepan over medium heat until browned. Add onion and garlic; cook until crisp-tender, stirring often. Stir in beans and next 5 ingredients. Bring to a boil; cover, reduce heat, and simmer 20 minutes, stirring occasionally.

Cook rice according to package directions, omitting salt and fat.

Remove and discard bay leaves. Spoon rice into individual bowls; top evenly with bean mixture. **Yield:** 4 servings (serving size: 1 cup rice and 1 cup bean mixture).

Per Serving:

Calories 409
Fat 4.8g (sat 1.3g)
Protein 15.5g
Carbohydrate 74.4g

Fiber 8.3g
Cholesterol 26mg
Sodium 601mg
Exchanges 4½ Starch, 1 Vegetable, ½ High-Fat Meat

Old-Fashioned Turkey Hash

Turkey Comparison: Ounce for ounce, white meat turkey has half the fat of dark meat.

Cooking spray
1   teaspoon vegetable oil
2   cups cubed cooked turkey breast
1   cup chopped onion (about 1 large)
1   (15-ounce) can sliced cooked potatoes, drained
⅔   cup fat-free milk
½   cup fat-free, less-sodium chicken broth
¼   teaspoon freshly ground black pepper
¼   teaspoon ground thyme
4   (¾-ounce) slices light wheat sandwich bread, toasted
Additional freshly ground black pepper (optional)

Coat a large nonstick skillet with cooking spray; add oil, and place over medium-high heat until hot. Add turkey, onion, and potatoes; cook 10 minutes or until onion is tender and potatoes are browned, stirring occasionally.

Add milk and next 3 ingredients to turkey mixture; bring to a boil. Reduce heat, and simmer, uncovered, 8 to 10 minutes or until desired consistency, stirring occasionally.

Cut slices of toast in half diagonally, and place on 4 individual serving plates. Spoon hash mixture evenly over toast. Sprinkle with additional pepper, if desired. **Yield:** 4 servings (serving size: about 1 cup hash and 1 slice toast).

Per Serving:

Calories 224	Fiber 4.9g
Fat 4.4g (sat 1.1g)	Cholesterol 27mg
Protein 25.3g	Sodium 1,054mg
Carbohydrate 21.4g	Exchanges 1½ Starch, 3 Very Lean Meat

SALADS

Chicken Salad, page 120

Cranberry Salad • Pineapple-Orange Congealed Salad
Waldorf Salad • Spinach Salad with Strawberries and Pecans
Caraway Coleslaw • Broccoli Salad • Mozzarella-Tomato Salad
Layered Vegetable Salad • Garden Potato Salad • Chicken Salad
Chicken Tenders Salad • Turkey and Grain Salad

Prep: 10 minutes   Chill: 45 minutes   Chill: 4 hours

Cranberry Salad

Holiday Favorite:
The flavor of this
dish will remind
you of a cranberry
congealed salad,
but the texture is
more like cranberry
sauce. We suggest
serving it with
roasted turkey
or ham.

1   (15¼-ounce) can crushed pineapple in juice
1   (3-ounce) package sugar-free raspberry-flavored gelatin
1   cup boiling water
½   (16-ounce) can whole-berry cranberry sauce
1½ cups diced apple
½   cup diced celery
⅓   cup chopped walnuts, toasted

Drain crushed pineapple, reserving ¾ cup juice; set aside.
Combine gelatin and boiling water in a bowl; stir until gelatin dissolves.
Stir in reserved pineapple juice and cranberry sauce. Cover and chill
45 minutes or until the consistency of unbeaten egg white. Fold in
drained pineapple, apple, celery, and walnuts.
Spoon gelatin mixture into a 1-quart serving bowl. Cover and chill
4 hours or until firm. **Yield:** 8 (½-cup) servings.

Per Serving:

Calories 150   Fiber 2.1g
Fat 3.0g (sat 0.2g)   Cholesterol 0mg
Protein 2.0g   Sodium 45mg
Carbohydrate 30.4g   Exchanges 1 Starch, 1 Fruit, ½ Fat

Prep: 5 minutes   Chill: 4 hours

Pineapple-Orange Congealed Salad

Dessert Option:
This congealed
fruit salad is sweet
enough to enjoy
for dessert. Also,
the recipe can
easily be halved
to serve six.

2   envelopes unflavored gelatin
2   cups orange juice, divided
2   cups crushed pineapple in juice, drained
4   packets calorie-free sweetener with aspartame
2   tablespoons fresh lemon juice
½   teaspoon almond extract
¼   teaspoon salt
Cooking spray

Soften gelatin in ½ cup orange juice. Bring remaining 1½ cups orange juice to a boil in a small saucepan; add to softened gelatin. Stir until gelatin dissolves.

Add pineapple and next 4 ingredients; stir well. Pour mixture into a 6-cup ring mold coated with cooking spray. Cover and chill 4 hours or until set. Unmold salad onto a serving platter. **Yield:** 12 (½-cup) servings.

Per Serving:

Calories 49	Fiber 0.4g
Fat 0.1g (sat 0.0g)	Cholesterol 0mg
Protein 1.3g	Sodium 55mg
Carbohydrate 10.5g	Exchange 1 Fruit

Prep: 14 minutes

Waldorf Salad

1½ cups coarsely chopped apple (about 1 medium)
1 cup coarsely chopped pear (about 1 medium)
1 cup seedless red grapes
½ cup thinly sliced celery
⅓ cup vanilla fat-free yogurt
1 tablespoon apple juice
¼ teaspoon ground ginger

Combine first 4 ingredients in a medium bowl. Combine yogurt, apple juice, and ginger; pour over apple mixture, tossing to coat. **Yield:** 6 (⅔-cup) servings.

Per Serving:

Calories 63	Fiber 1.8g
Fat 0.5g (sat 0.2g)	Cholesterol 1mg
Protein 1.0g	Sodium 15mg
Carbohydrate 15.2g	Exchange 1 Fruit

Grapes Pack a Punch:
Red grapes contain an antioxidant called resveratrol that may help lower cholesterol and reduce the risk of heart disease. Red wine contains resveratrol, too.

super
quick

vegetarian

Spinach Salad with Strawberries and Pecans

3	tablespoons cider vinegar or white vinegar
3	tablespoons vegetable oil
2	tablespoons "measures-like-sugar" calorie-free sweetener
1½	teaspoons Dijon mustard
½	teaspoon salt
¼	teaspoon pepper
½	small onion, coarsely chopped
1	teaspoon poppy seeds
1	(10-ounce) package fresh spinach, torn
1	cup strawberries, halved
⅓	cup pecan halves, toasted

Combine first 7 ingredients in a blender; process until smooth, stopping once to scrape down sides. Stir in poppy seeds.
Combine spinach, strawberries, and pecans; drizzle with poppy seed dressing. **Yield:** 6 (1-cup) servings.

Per Serving:

Calories 138	**Fiber** 2.5g
Fat 11.6g (sat 0.9g)	**Cholesterol** 0mg
Protein 2.5g	**Sodium** 265mg
Carbohydrate 10.2g	**Exchanges** 1 Vegetable, ½ Fruit, 2 Fat

Heart Smart: This salad just might keep your heart healthy. Spinach is a top source of beta-carotene, which appears to reduce the risk of heart disease. Strawberries contain vitamin C, which also can help prevent heart disease. And pecans are packed with heart-healthy mono-unsaturated fat.

Prep: 15 minutes

Caraway Coleslaw

Salad Shortcut:
Instead of shredding
your own cabbage,
buy a package
of preshredded
cabbage or coleslaw
mix (without the
dressing packet). A
10-ounce package
of preshredded
cabbage or coleslaw
contains about
6 cups.

3 cups shredded cabbage
½ cup chopped green bell pepper
⅓ cup light mayonnaise
1 tablespoon white vinegar
½ teaspoon sugar
½ teaspoon caraway seeds
¼ teaspoon seasoned salt

Combine cabbage and pepper. Combine mayonnaise and remaining ingredients, stirring well. Pour mayonnaise mixture over cabbage. Toss well. Cover and chill. **Yield:** 6 (½-cup) servings.

Per Serving:

Calories 63	Fiber 0.8g
Fat 4.6g (sat 0.9g)	Cholesterol 4mg
Protein 0.5g	Sodium 171mg
Carbohydrate 5.3g	Exchanges 1 Vegetable, 1 Fat

Broccoli Salad

8	cups broccoli florets
1	cup chopped red onion
½	cup sunflower kernels
½	cup raisins
1	cup fat-free mayonnaise
2	tablespoons white vinegar
1	tablespoon "measures-like-sugar" calorie-free sweetener
4	bacon slices, cooked and crumbled

Nutrition Note: *Using regular bacon in small amounts is not a "no-no" when you're trying to lose weight. One slice of regular bacon has only about 35 calories and 3 grams of fat.*

Combine first 4 ingredients in a large bowl. Combine mayonnaise, vinegar, and sweetener, stirring well. Pour dressing over broccoli mixture; stir gently. Cover and chill thoroughly. Sprinkle with bacon and toss gently before serving. **Yield:** 14 (½-cup) servings.

Per Serving:

Calories 87	Fiber 2.0g
Fat 3.8g (sat 0.6g)	Cholesterol 2mg
Protein 2.6g	Sodium 161mg
Carbohydrate 13.4g	Exchanges 1 Vegetable, ½ Fruit, ½ Fat

Prep: 10 minutes

Mozzarella-Tomato Salad

Tomato Time:
*This simple salad is
best in the summer
when juicy, fresh-
from-the-garden
tomatoes are
available. When
selecting tomatoes,
look for those that
are firm and
well-shaped, and
have brightly
colored skin. They
should be heavy
for their size and
blemish-free.*

2 large red tomatoes, each cut into 4 slices
6 (1-ounce) slices part-skim mozzarella cheese, each cut in half
12 large basil leaves
2 large yellow tomatoes, each cut into 4 slices
3 tablespoons fat-free balsamic vinaigrette
1 teaspoon freshly ground black pepper

Stack 4 tomato slices, 3 cheese slices, and 3 basil leaves in each of 4 stacks, alternating tomato, cheese, and basil.
Drizzle stacks evenly with vinaigrette. Cover and chill. Sprinkle with pepper before serving. **Yield:** 4 servings.

Per Serving:

Calories 165	Fiber 1.9g
Fat 7.9g (sat 4.7g)	Cholesterol 23mg
Protein 14.0g	Sodium 407mg
Carbohydrate 11.4g	Exchanges 2 Vegetable, 1 High-Fat Meat

Prep: 15 minutes

Layered Vegetable Salad

Salad Shortcut:

For bacon in a flash, cook it in the microwave. Place bacon slices on a microwave-safe plate or bacon rack, cover with paper towels and cook at HIGH about 1 minute per slice until crisp.

4   cups torn iceberg lettuce
1   cup chopped celery
1   (10-ounce) package frozen green peas, thawed
1   cup chopped red onion
1   cup chopped green bell pepper
¾   cup light mayonnaise
¾   cup fat-free sour cream
3   turkey bacon slices, cooked and crumbled
½   cup (2 ounces) shredded reduced-fat Cheddar cheese

Layer lettuce, celery, peas, onion, and green bell pepper in a 2-quart bowl.

Combine mayonnaise and sour cream, stirring well. Spread mixture over top of salad. Sprinkle bacon around edges of mayonnaise mixture, and sprinkle cheese in center. Cover and chill. Toss before serving.
Yield: 8 (1-cup) servings.

Per Serving:

Calories 177	Fiber 3.0g
Fat 10.3g (sat 2.4g)	Cholesterol 20mg
Protein 6.8g	Sodium 374mg
Carbohydrate 14.7g	Exchanges 3 Vegetable, 2 Fat

Prep: 4 minutes   Cook: 20 minutes   Chill: 2 hours

Garden Potato Salad

3   round red potatoes (about 1 pound)
1   cup frozen cut green beans
1   cup frozen whole-kernel corn
⅓   cup chopped red bell pepper
⅓   cup thinly sliced green onions
½   cup fat-free sour cream
2   tablespoons light mayonnaise
½   teaspoon salt
½   teaspoon black pepper
½   teaspoon dried oregano
¼   teaspoon ground cumin

Nutrition Note:
When you use fat-free and low-fat versions of sour cream and mayonnaise in potato salad, you reduce the fat by more than half.

Peel potatoes, and cut into cubes. Place potato in saucepan; add water to cover. Bring to a boil; cover, reduce heat, and simmer, 15 minutes or until tender. Drain and cool.

Place green beans and corn in a saucepan; add water to cover. Bring to a boil; cover, reduce heat, and simmer, 5 minutes or until beans are crisp-tender. Drain and cool.

Combine potato, green beans and corn, red bell pepper, and green onions in a bowl. Combine sour cream and remaining 5 ingredients; stir well. Pour sour cream mixture over potato mixture and toss well. Cover and chill at least 2 hours. **Yield:** 6 (⅔-cup) servings.

Per Serving:

Calories 111	Fiber 2.7g
Fat 1.6g (sat 0.3g)	Cholesterol 2mg
Protein 4.0g	Sodium 255mg
Carbohydrate 21.1g	Exchanges 1 Starch, 1 Vegetable

Prep: 15 minutes   Chill: 1 hour

Chicken Salad

Chicken Choices:

*This salad is a
great use of leftover
chicken. But if you
don't have leftover
chicken, here are
some other options.*

- *Frozen cooked
  diced chicken*

- *Refrigerated
  grilled chicken
  strips*

- *Deli-roasted
  chicken (remove
  skin; use white
  meat)*

*You'll need
about a pound of
cooked chicken
(meat only) to get
3 cups of chopped.*

3	cups chopped cooked chicken breast
1	cup thinly sliced celery
2	tablespoons lemon juice
1	tablespoon minced onion
½	cup light mayonnaise
½	teaspoon pepper
¼	teaspoon salt
½	cup seedless green grapes, halved lengthwise
½	cup seedless red grapes, halved lengthwise
1	(2-ounce) package sliced almonds, toasted

Bibb lettuce (optional)

Combine first 4 ingredients; cover and chill at least 1 hour.

Combine mayonnaise, pepper, and salt. Add mayonnaise mixture, grapes, and almonds to chilled chicken mixture; toss gently. Serve chicken salad on lettuce leaves, if desired. **Yield:** 6 servings (serving size: about 1 cup).

Per Serving:

Calories 254	Fiber 1.7g
Fat 13.7g (sat 2.0g)	Cholesterol 61mg
Protein 22.8g	Sodium 319mg
Carbohydrate 9.7g	Exchanges ½ Fruit, 3 Lean Meat, 1 Fat

(Photograph on page 107)

Chicken Tenders Salad

¼   cup all-purpose flour
½   teaspoon pepper
1   pound chicken tenders
3   tablespoons egg substitute
⅓   cup fat-free milk
1   cup Italian-seasoned breadcrumbs
3   tablespoons sesame seeds
Cooking spray
1   (10-ounce) package romaine lettuce, torn
2   large tomatoes, cut into wedges
½   red onion, sliced (about 1½ cups)
¼   cup (1 ounce) shredded reduced-fat Cheddar cheese
¼   cup light ranch dressing

Fat Comparison: Compare the oven-fried chicken fingers in this salad to those you get at a fast-food chicken restaurant. The oven-fried version has 2 grams of fat per 3-ounce serving; fast-food chicken fingers have 16 grams of fat.

Preheat oven to 425°. Combine flour and pepper in a heavy-duty zip-top plastic bag. Add chicken; seal bag, and shake to coat.

Combine egg substitute and milk in a shallow dish, stirring well. Combine breadcrumbs and sesame seeds in a shallow dish.

Dip each chicken tender in egg mixture, and dredge in breadcrumb mixture. Place in a single layer on a baking sheet coated with cooking spray. Coat chicken tenders with cooking spray. Bake, uncovered, at 425° for 20 minutes or until done. Cut chicken tenders diagonally into 1-inch pieces.

Place 2 cups lettuce on each of 4 individual serving plates. Divide chicken, tomato, and onion evenly among plates. Top each serving with 1 tablespoon cheese. Serve with ranch dressing. **Yield:** 4 servings.

Per Serving:

Calories 396	Fiber 4.5g
Fat 6.5g (sat 1.4g)	Cholesterol 72mg
Protein 37.3g	Sodium 856mg
Carbohydrate 35.3g	Exchanges 2 Starch, 1 Vegetable, 4 Very Lean Meat, 1 Fat

Prep: 10 minutes   Cook: 45 minutes   Chill: 3 hours

Turkey and Grain Salad

Go with the Grain:
Wild rice and
barley are two
excellent sources
of fiber—a nutrient
that helps in blood
sugar control.

6	cups water
¾	cup uncooked wild rice
½	cup uncooked pearl barley
½	pound smoked turkey breast, diced
2	cups diced Red Delicious apple
¾	cup sliced green onions
¾	cup diced celery
⅓	cup cider vinegar
¼	cup thawed apple juice concentrate, undiluted
1	tablespoon olive oil
1	tablespoon Dijon mustard
1	teaspoon dried thyme
½	teaspoon freshly ground black pepper
12	red leaf lettuce leaves

Combine water, wild rice, and barley in a large saucepan; bring to a boil. Cover, reduce heat, and simmer 45 minutes or until rice and barley are tender. Drain. Add turkey and next 3 ingredients; toss well.

Combine vinegar and next 5 ingredients. Pour over rice mixture; toss well. Cover and chill 3 hours, stirring occasionally.

To serve, place 2 lettuce leaves on each of 6 plates. Spoon rice mixture over lettuce. **Yield:** 6 (1½-cup) servings.

Per Serving:

Calories 295	Fiber 6.2g
Fat 4.7g (sat 0.8g)	Cholesterol 22mg
Protein 17.4g	Sodium 412mg
Carbohydrate 50.6g	Exchanges 3 Starch, 1 Vegetable, 1 Lean Meat

SIDE DISHES

Corn, Okra, and Tomatoes, page 131

Prep: 15 minutes   Cook: 30 minutes

Skillet Apples

Make a Meal:
Serve these sweet,
tender apples as a
side dish for
roasted pork or
turkey. They're also
good for breakfast
along with a bowl
of oatmeal or with
eggs, bacon, and
toast.

1   tablespoon light butter
9   Granny Smith apples, peeled, cored, and cut into wedges
½   teaspoon ground cinnamon
1   tablespoon "measures-like-sugar" brown sugar calorie-free
        sweetener

Melt butter in a large nonstick skillet over medium heat; stir in apple and remaining ingredients. Bring to a boil; cover, reduce heat, and simmer 30 minutes or until tender, stirring occasionally. **Yield:** 8 (½-cup) servings.

Per Serving:

Calories 91	**Fiber** 2.8g
Fat 1.2g (sat 0.6g)	**Cholesterol** 3mg
Protein 0.4g	**Sodium** 9mg
Carbohydrate 23.0g	**Exchanges** 1½ Fruit

Prep: 5 minutes   Cook: 10 minutes

Curried Baked Pineapple

2   (20-ounce) cans pineapple chunks in juice, drained
15   reduced-fat round buttery crackers, crushed
¼   cup packed brown sugar
¼   cup (1 ounce) shredded reduced-fat sharp Cheddar cheese
½   teaspoon curry powder
Fat-free butter spray (such as I Can't Believe It's Not Butter!)

Preheat oven to 450°.
Place pineapple chunks in an 11 x 7-inch baking dish; set aside.
Combine cracker crumbs and next 3 ingredients. Sprinkle cracker mixture over pineapple. Coat cracker mixture with butter spray. Bake at 450° for 10 minutes or until lightly browned. **Yield:** 8 servings (serving size: about ⅔ cup).

Per Serving:

Calories 118	Fiber 0.0g
Fat 1.4g (sat 0.4g)	Cholesterol 2mg
Protein 1.4g	Sodium 82mg
Carbohydrate 24.6g	Exchanges ½ Starch, 1 Fruit

*Dessert Treat:
This sweet fruit
side dish is so
scrumptious (and
so easy) that you
might want to have
it for dessert. It's a
great way to add
fruit to your meal.*

Prep: 5 minutes   Cook: 37 minutes

Butter Beans with Bacon and Green Onions

2	(10-ounce) packages frozen butter beans
4	reduced-fat bacon slices (such as Gwaltney's)
4	green onions, chopped
2	garlic cloves, minced
½	cup chopped fresh parsley
½	teaspoon salt
½	teaspoon pepper
1	tablespoon balsamic vinegar (optional)

Flavor Secret: Balsamic vinegar adds a distinctive tangy sweetness to foods, and, like other vinegars, it's calorie-free.

Cook butter beans according to package direction, omitting salt and fat; set aside.

Cook bacon in a large nonstick skillet over medium-high heat until crisp; remove bacon, reserving drippings in pan. Crumble bacon, and set aside.

Cook green onions and garlic in bacon drippings until tender, stirring often. Stir in beans, parsley, salt, pepper, and, if desired, vinegar. Cook just until heated. Sprinkle with crumbled bacon. **Yield:** 8 (½-cup) servings.

Per Serving:

Calories 95	**Fiber** 4.6g
Fat 1.0g (sat 0.3g)	**Cholesterol** 3mg
Protein 6.0g	**Sodium** 265mg
Carbohydrate 15.6g	**Exchange** 1 Starch

Old-Fashioned Baked Beans

Test Kitchen Secret:
To test the baked
beans for doneness,
you can spear a
couple of them
with a fork or you
can press 1 or 2
beans between your
fingers to feel how
tender they are.

1	(16-ounce) package dried navy beans
1½	quarts water
2	cups chopped onion
1	cup ketchup
½	cup chopped lean cooked ham
¼	cup molasses
1	tablespoon prepared mustard
½	teaspoon salt
½	teaspoon pepper

Cooking spray

Sort and wash beans; place beans in a large Dutch oven. Cover with water to a depth of 2 inches above beans; soak overnight. Drain and rinse beans.

Combine beans, 1½ quarts water, and chopped onion in pan. Bring to a boil; cover, reduce heat, and simmer 2 hours. Drain bean mixture, reserving 2 cups cooking liquid.

Preheat oven to 350°.

Combine bean mixture, reserved cooking liquid, ketchup, and next 5 ingredients in a large bowl; stir well. Pour mixture into a 3-quart casserole coated with cooking spray. Bake, uncovered, at 350° for 1 hour and 30 minutes or until beans are tender. **Yield:** 15 (½-cup) servings.

Per Serving:

Calories 145	Fiber 5.1g
Fat 0.8g (sat 0.2g)	Cholesterol 2mg
Protein 7.4g	Sodium 351mg
Carbohydrate 28.5g	Exchanges 2 Starch

Prep: 15 minutes   Cook: 30 minutes

Green Bean Casserole

Cooking spray
1   teaspoon vegetable oil
½   cup chopped onion
½   cup chopped fresh mushrooms
2   (10-ounce) packages frozen French-style green beans, thawed
         and drained
1   (10¾-ounce) can condensed reduced-fat, reduced-sodium
         cream of mushroom soup, undiluted
¼   cup fat-free milk
2   teaspoons low-sodium soy sauce
¼   teaspoon pepper
¼   cup crushed garlic-flavored croutons

Preheat oven to 375°.

Heat oil in a large skillet coated with cooking spray; add onion and mushrooms. Cook 3 to 4 minutes or until onion is golden. Remove from heat, and stir in green beans.

Combine soup and next 3 ingredients, stirring with a whisk until smooth; add to green bean mixture. Stir well.

Spoon mixture into a 1½-quart baking dish coated with cooking spray. Bake, uncovered, at 375° for 25 minutes; sprinkle with crushed croutons. Bake an additional 5 minutes or until bubbly. **Yield:** 6 (½-cup) servings.

Lighten Up:

Our green bean casserole is lower in fat, calories, and sodium than a traditional version because we used reduced-fat, reduced-sodium cream soup and fat-free milk, and topped it with croutons instead of fried onion rings.

Per Serving:

Calories 79	Fiber 2.1g
Fat 2.5g (sat 0.6g)	Cholesterol 2mg
Protein 2.4g	Sodium 281mg
Carbohydrate 11.5g	Exchanges ½ Starch, 1 Vegetable, 1 Fat

Prep: 15 minutes   Cook: 23 minutes

Broccoli Casserole

2   (10-ounce) packages frozen chopped broccoli
½   cup water
1   (10¾-ounce) can condensed reduced-fat, reduced-sodium
        cream of mushroom soup, undiluted
1   (8-ounce) can sliced water chestnuts, drained
⅓   cup minced onion
¼   teaspoon salt
Cooking spray
⅔   cup (2.6 ounces) shredded reduced-fat Cheddar cheese

Preheat oven to 350°.

Combine broccoli and water in a 1½-quart baking dish. Cover with heavy-duty plastic wrap and vent. Microwave at HIGH 7 to 9 minutes or until tender. Drain well to remove excess moisture.

Combine broccoli, soup, and next 3 ingredients in a medium bowl; stir well. Spoon into a 1½-quart baking dish coated with cooking spray.

Cover and bake at 350° for 20 minutes or until bubbly. Uncover and sprinkle with cheese; bake an additional 2 to 3 minutes or until cheese melts. **Yield:** 8 (½-cup) servings.

Per Serving:

Calories 80	Fiber 2.3g
Fat 2.8g (sat 1.4g)	Cholesterol 7mg
Protein 5.3g	Sodium 304mg
Carbohydrate 9.4g	Exchanges 2 Vegetable, ½ Fat

Prep: 15 minutes   Cook: 35 minutes

Corn, Okra, and Tomatoes

¼   cup margarine
1   large onion, chopped
1   large green bell pepper, chopped
2   garlic cloves, minced
2   cups chopped plum tomato
2½   cups fresh corn kernels (about 5 ears)
1   cup sliced fresh okra
½   teaspoon salt
½   teaspoon freshly ground black pepper

Fresh or Frozen:
If fresh corn is not
in season, use
2½ cups frozen
yellow corn.

Melt margarine in a nonstick skillet over medium-high heat. Add onion, bell pepper, and garlic; sauté 5 minutes or until tender. Add chopped tomato; bring to a boil. Reduce heat, and simmer, uncovered, 15 minutes.

Add corn and remaining ingredients; bring to a boil. Reduce heat, and simmer 9 minutes or until corn is tender. **Yield:** 6 servings (serving size: about 1 cup).

Per Serving:

Calories 162	Fiber 4.1g
Fat 7.5g (sat 1.5g)	Cholesterol 0mg
Protein 3.7g	Sodium 280mg
Carbohydrate 23.8g	Exchanges 1 Starch, 1 Vegetable, 1 Fat

(Photograph on page 123)

Prep: 10 minutes   Cook: 1 hour

Fresh Corn Pudding

2   cups fresh corn kernels (about 4 ears)
1   tablespoon minced green bell pepper
1½ tablespoons all-purpose flour
2   teaspoons sugar
¼   teaspoon salt
¼   teaspoon mace
Dash of ground red pepper
½   cup egg substitute
1   cup fat-free evaporated milk
Cooking spray

Preheat oven to 350°.

Combine first 7 ingredients, stirring well. Combine egg substitute and evaporated milk; add to corn mixture.

Spoon mixture into a 1-quart baking dish coated with cooking spray. Place dish in a large shallow pan; add water to pan to a depth of 1 inch. Bake at 350° for 1 hour or until a knife inserted in center comes out clean. **Yield:** 6 servings (serving size: about ⅔ cup).

Nutrition Note: We replaced two whole eggs with ½ cup egg substitute. The egg substitute has no fat or cholesterol, compared to about 10 grams of fat and 420 milligrams of cholesterol for two eggs.

Per Serving:

Calories 116	**Fiber** 1.6g
Fat 0.8g (sat 0.1g)	**Cholesterol** 3mg
Protein 6.7g	**Sodium** 202mg
Carbohydrate 22.4g	**Exchanges** 1½ Starch

Yellow Squash Casserole

Eat Your Veggies:
Foods that are dark
green, deep orange,
or bright yellow
(such as yellow
squash) are high
in beta-carotene—
a substance in food
that reduces the
risk of heart disease
and may protect
against cataracts.

2   pounds yellow squash, sliced
1   cup chopped onion
1   teaspoon reduced-calorie margarine, melted
9   reduced-fat round buttery crackers, crushed and divided
¼   cup (1 ounce) shredded reduced-fat sharp Cheddar cheese
2   lower-sodium bacon slices, cooked and crumbled
1   (2-ounce) jar diced pimiento, drained
1   large egg, lightly beaten
1   large egg white
¼   teaspoon salt
¼   teaspoon pepper
Cooking spray

Preheat oven to 350°.

Combine squash and water to cover in a large Dutch oven; bring to a boil. Cover, reduce heat, and simmer 5 minutes or until squash is tender. Drain well, and mash; set aside.

Cook onion in margarine until tender. Combine onion, squash, ⅓ cup cracker crumbs, and next 7 ingredients. Spoon into a 2-quart baking dish coated with cooking spray. Sprinkle with remaining cracker crumbs. Bake, uncovered, at 350° for 45 minutes. **Yield:** 6 (½-cup) servings.

Per Serving:

Calories 109	Fiber 3.1g
Fat 4.6g (sat 1.5g)	Cholesterol 43mg
Protein 6.3g	Sodium 241mg
Carbohydrate 12.5g	Exchanges 2½ Vegetable, 1 Fat

Prep: 20 minutes   Cook: 16 minutes

Turnip Greens with Canadian Bacon

Seasoning Secret:

Instead of cooking your greens with a piece of fatback, add flavor with lean Canadian bacon, roasted red bell pepper, and balsamic vinegar. The fat savings are significant, and the flavor is phenomenal.

Olive oil-flavored cooking spray
1   (6-ounce) package Canadian bacon, cut into ½-inch pieces
2   (16-ounce) packages fresh turnip greens, coarsely chopped
¼   cup water
1   cup bottled roasted red bell pepper, drained and chopped
2   tablespoons balsamic vinegar
½   teaspoon salt
¼   teaspoon freshly ground black pepper

Coat a large Dutch oven with cooking spray, and place over medium-high heat until hot. Add Canadian bacon and cook 3 to 4 minutes or until lightly browned.

Add turnip greens and water; bring to a boil. Cover, reduce heat to low, and cook 10 minutes or until turnip greens are tender. Stir in bell pepper and remaining ingredients. Cover, and simmer 3 minutes. **Yield:** 8 (½-cup) servings.

Per Serving:

Calories 69	Fiber 2.9g
Fat 2.0g (sat 0.6g)	Cholesterol 11mg
Protein 6.3g	Sodium 819mg
Carbohydrate 7.9g	Exchanges 1½ Vegetable, ½ Lean Meat

Prep: 12 minutes   Cook: 15 minutes

Cheese Fries

1½ pounds baking potatoes, unpeeled and cut into thin strips
          (about 3 potatoes)
Cooking spray
¼   cup grated Parmesan cheese
¼   teaspoon salt
¼   teaspoon pepper
¼   teaspoon paprika

Preheat oven to 450°.

Coat potato strips with cooking spray, and place in a large heavy-duty zip-top plastic bag.

Combine cheese and remaining 3 ingredients; sprinkle over potato strips in bag. Seal bag and turn to coat potatoes well.

Arrange potato strips in a single layer on a large baking sheet or jelly roll pan coated with cooking spray. Bake at 450° for 15 minutes, turning once. Serve immediately. **Yield:** 6 servings.

Per Serving:

Calories 147	Fiber 2.1g
Fat 1.7g (sat 0.9g)	Cholesterol 4mg
Protein 4.4g	Sodium 190mg
Carbohydrate 28.9g	Exchanges 2 Starch

(Photograph on page 163)

Fat Comparison: One serving of these oven-baked fries has only 1.7 grams of fat compared to 12 grams of fat in a small order of fast-food French fries.

Hearty Mashed Potatoes

3   large Yukon gold potatoes, peeled and cut into 1-inch cubes
3   lower-sodium bacon slices, chopped
4   cups thinly sliced green cabbage
½   cup fat-free, less-sodium chicken broth
¼   cup fat-free milk
¼   cup low-fat sour cream
½   teaspoon salt
¼   teaspoon pepper
¼   cup sliced green onions

Cook potato in boiling water to cover 20 to 25 minutes or until tender. Drain well.

Cook bacon in a large skillet over medium heat 3 minutes or until browned. Add cabbage and chicken broth. Bring to a boil; cover, reduce heat, and simmer 10 minutes. Uncover, increase heat to high, and cook 2 minutes or until most of the liquid is absorbed.

Combine potato, milk, sour cream, salt, and pepper. Mash with a potato masher or beat with a mixer at medium speed until smooth. Add cabbage mixture and green onions; stir well. **Yield:** 8 (½-cup) servings.

Per Serving:

Calories 160

Fat 3.6g (sat 1.5g)

Protein 6.0g

Carbohydrate 26.3g

Fiber 3.3g

Cholesterol 8mg

Sodium 485mg

Exchanges 1½ Starch, ½ Vegetable, ½ Fat

Prep: 10 minutes   Cook: 30 minutes

Sweet Potatoes in Orange Syrup

2¼ pounds sweet potatoes, peeled and cut into ¼-inch-thick slices
Butter-flavored cooking spray
¼ cup reduced-calorie maple syrup
1 tablespoon frozen orange juice concentrate
2 tablespoons coarsely chopped pecans, toasted

Preheat oven to 375°.

Place potato slices, overlapping slightly, on a jelly roll pan coated with cooking spray. Coat potato with cooking spray. Bake, uncovered, at 375° for 30 minutes or until tender, turning once. Transfer to a bowl.

Combine syrup, juice concentrate, and pecans in a glass measure. Microwave at HIGH 30 seconds; drizzle over potato slices. **Yield:** 8 (½-cup) servings.

Sweet Potatoes:
Sweet potatoes are one holiday food you certainly don't need to give up. They're packed with fiber, iron, and vitamins A, C, and E.

Per Serving:

Calories 141
Fat 2.0g (sat 0.2g)
Protein 2.0g
Carbohydrate 29.7g

Fiber 3.5g
Cholesterol 0mg
Sodium 17mg
Exchanges 2 Starch

Prep: 20 minutes   Cook: 30 minutes

Sweet Potato Casserole

Microwave Tip:
To get 3 cups
cooked mashed
sweet potato,
you can cook 3
medium-size sweet
potatoes in the
microwave at HIGH
9 to 11 minutes or
until tender.

3   cups mashed cooked sweet potato (about 2¼ pounds)
3   tablespoons "measures-like-sugar" brown sugar calorie-free
         sweetener
¼   cup fat-free milk
1   tablespoon orange juice
1   tablespoon reduced-calorie stick margarine, melted
1   teaspoon vanilla extract
½   teaspoon salt
2   large egg whites, lightly beaten
Butter-flavored cooking spray
⅓   cup "measures-like-sugar" brown sugar calorie-free sweetener
¼   cup all-purpose flour
2   tablespoons chilled reduced-calorie stick margarine
⅓   cup chopped pecans

Preheat oven to 350°.
Combine first 8 ingredients in a medium bowl. Spoon potato mixture
into an 8-inch square baking dish coated with cooking spray.
Combine ⅓ cup sweetener and flour; cut in 2 tablespoons chilled margarine with a pastry blender or 2 knives until mixture resembles coarse
meal. Stir in chopped pecans; sprinkle over top of casserole. Lightly
coat top of casserole with cooking spray. Bake at 350° for 30 minutes.
Yield: 8 (½-cup) servings.

Per Serving:

Calories 226	Fiber 2.8g
Fat 6.1g (sat 0.8g)	Cholesterol 0mg
Protein 4.1g	Sodium 232mg
Carbohydrate 46.8g	Exchanges 3 Starch, 1 Fat

Lighten Up:

Compare our sweet potato casserole to a traditional version:

½-cup serving	Traditional	Light
Calories	592	226
Fat	32.1g	6.1g
Carbohydrate	73.1g	46.8g

Prep: 15 minutes   Cook: 35 minutes

Macaroni and Cheese

Main Attraction:
Enjoy this cheesy
pasta as your main
dish instead of a
side dish. It's got
plenty of protein,
so all you'll need
to add is a green
salad and a piece
of fruit.

1   (8-ounce) package elbow macaroni
2   cups (8 ounces) shredded reduced-fat sharp Cheddar cheese
1   cup 1% low-fat cottage cheese
¾   cup fat-free sour cream
½   cup fat-free milk
2   tablespoons grated fresh onion
1½   teaspoons reduced-calorie margarine, melted
½   teaspoon salt
¼   teaspoon pepper
1   large egg, lightly beaten
Butter-flavored cooking spray
¼   cup dry breadcrumbs
1   tablespoon reduced-calorie margarine, melted
¼   teaspoon paprika

Cook macaroni according to package directions, omitting salt and fat. Drain well.

Preheat oven to 350°.

Combine macaroni, Cheddar cheese, and next 8 ingredients; spoon into a 2-quart baking dish coated with cooking spray. Combine breadcrumbs, 1 tablespoon melted margarine, and paprika; sprinkle over casserole. Cover and bake at 350° for 30 minutes. Uncover; bake an additional 5 minutes or until set. **Yield:** 6 (1-cup) servings.

Per Serving:

Calories 356	Fiber 1.2g
Fat 11.2g (sat 5.9g)	Cholesterol 63mg
Protein 24.9g	Sodium 724mg
Carbohydrate 37.5g	Exchanges 2½ Starch, 2 Medium-Fat Meat

Prep: 3 minutes   Cook: 5 minutes

Garlic-Herb Cheese Grits

Ingredient
Substitution:
If you can't find
garlic-and-spices
cream cheese, use
light cream cheese
and stir in 1 or 2
teaspoons of a
garlic-and-herb
seasoning blend.

2   (16-ounce) cans fat-free, less-sodium chicken broth
1   cup uncooked quick-cooking grits
1   (6-ounce) package garlic-and-spices light cream cheese
¼   teaspoon pepper

Bring broth to a boil in a medium saucepan over high heat; gradually stir in grits. Cook, stirring constantly, 5 to 7 minutes or until thick.
Remove grits from heat, and stir in cream cheese and pepper. Serve immediately. **Yield:** 6 (¾-cup) servings.

Per Serving:

Calories 170

Fat 5.2g (sat 3.0g)

Protein 6.8g

Carbohydrate 23.5g

Fiber 1.3g

Cholesterol 20mg

Sodium 182mg

Exchanges 1½ Starch, 1 Fat

SOUPS & SANDWICHES

Smoked Chicken Club Sandwiches, page 161

Fresh Tomato Soup • Macaroni and Cheese Soup • Vegetable-Beef Soup

Beef Stew with Ale • Old-Fashioned Chicken-and-Rice Soup

Chicken-Corn Chowder • Dump-and-Stir Chili • Shrimp Gumbo

Grilled Cheese Sandwiches Deluxe • Canadian BLTs • Dagwood Sandwich

Tuna Salad Sandwiches • Smoked Chicken Club Sandwiches

Classic Hamburgers • Saucy Dogs

Fresh Tomato Soup

For A Quick Meal:
Serve with Grilled
Cheese Sandwiches
Deluxe (page 157).
This soup is pictured
on page 156.

1⅓ pounds fresh tomatoes (about 4 medium)
⅔ cup water
⅓ cup chopped onion
1¼ cups fat-free, less-sodium chicken broth
1 (8-ounce) can no-salt-added tomato sauce
½ teaspoon sugar
¼ teaspoon salt
⅛ teaspoon pepper
1½ tablespoons chopped fresh basil
Low-fat sour cream (optional)
Chopped green onions (optional)

With a knife, make a shallow X on bottom of each tomato. Dip tomatoes into a large pot of boiling water to blanch 30 seconds or just until skins begin to crack. Plunge immediately into ice water. Remove from water; pull skin away, using a sharp paring knife. Gently remove seeds; chop tomato.

Combine ⅔ cup water and onion in a large saucepan. Bring to a boil; reduce heat, and simmer, uncovered, 5 minutes. Stir in tomato, chicken broth, and next 4 ingredients. Bring to a boil; cover, reduce heat, and simmer 25 minutes. Stir in basil. Simmer, uncovered, 5 minutes. Set aside; cool 10 minutes.

Place half of mixture in a blender; process until smooth. Repeat with remaining mixture. Return to pan. Cook 3 to 4 minutes. Garnish with sour cream and chopped green onions, if desired. **Yield:** 4 (1-cup) servings.

Per Serving:

Calories 66	Fiber 2.9g
Fat 0.6g (sat 0.1g)	Cholesterol 0mg
Protein 2.2g	Sodium 349mg
Carbohydrate 13.9g	Exchanges 3 Vegetable

Prep: 10 minutes   Cook: 15 minutes

Macaroni and Cheese Soup

1	cup uncooked elbow macaroni
2	tablespoons margarine
½	cup finely chopped carrot
½	cup finely chopped celery
1	small onion, finely chopped
4	cups 1% low-fat milk
1	tablespoon chicken-flavored bouillon granules
½	teaspoon ground white pepper
2	tablespoons cornstarch
2	tablespoons water
6	ounces reduced-fat loaf process cheese spread, cubed
1	cup frozen whole-kernel corn
½	cup frozen green peas

Test Kitchen Secret: We use 1% low-fat milk instead of fat-free for most cream soups. The rich, creamy taste is worth the extra grams of fat.

Cook macaroni according to package directions, omitting salt and fat; drain. Rinse with cold water; drain and set aside.

Melt margarine in a large skillet over medium-high heat. Add carrot, celery, and onion; sauté until tender. Remove vegetable mixture from heat; set aside.

Combine milk, bouillon granules, and white pepper in a saucepan. Combine cornstarch and water, stirring until smooth; stir into milk mixture. Stir in vegetable mixture; cook over medium heat, stirring constantly, until mixture thickens and comes to a boil. Boil 1 minute, stirring constantly.

Add cheese, and cook over medium heat until cheese melts, stirring often.

Add macaroni, corn, and peas; cook over low heat, stirring constantly, just until thoroughly heated. **Yield:** 7 (1-cup) servings.

Per Serving:

Calories 181	Fiber 1.7g
Fat 8.1g (sat 3.4g)	Cholesterol 6mg
Protein 12.3g	Sodium 839mg
Carbohydrate 25.0g	Exchanges 1 Starch, 2 Vegetable, 1 High-Fat Meat

Prep: 35 minutes   Cook: 1 hour 45 minutes

Vegetable-Beef Soup

Stock Up:
Make a pot of soup
and save it for a
rainy day. Place the
soup in an
airtight container
or heavy-duty
zip-top plastic bag,
and freeze up to
1 month.

1½ pounds lean boneless chuck roast, trimmed
2   quarts water
1   teaspoon salt
1   teaspoon pepper
1   bay leaf
4   round red potatoes, peeled and cubed
4   carrots, scraped and chopped
2   cups chopped onion (about 2)
2   (8-ounce) cans no-salt-added tomato sauce
1   dried red chile pepper
2   cups coarsely chopped cabbage (about ½ small head)
1   (10-ounce) package frozen whole-kernel corn
1   (10-ounce) package frozen lima beans

Combine first 5 ingredients in a stockpot or large Dutch oven. Bring to a boil; cover, reduce heat, and simmer 1 hour. Remove meat, reserving liquid in pan; remove and discard bay leaf. Let meat cool. Chop meat. Skim fat from liquid in pan, if necessary.

Add chopped meat, potato, and next 4 ingredients to pan. Bring to a boil; cover, reduce heat, and simmer 30 minutes. Add cabbage, corn, and beans; cover and simmer 15 minutes or until vegetables are tender. Remove and discard chile pepper. **Yield:** 11 (2-cup) servings.

Per Serving:

Calories 244	**Fiber** 4.5g
Fat 10.6g (sat 4.1g)	**Cholesterol** 42mg
Protein 15.6g	**Sodium** 280mg
Carbohydrate 21.6g	**Exchanges** 1 Starch, 1 Vegetable, 2 Medium-Fat Meat

Beef Stew with Ale

Alcohol Alternative:

Because the stew simmers for over an hour, all of the alcohol in the ale evaporates, leaving only the robust flavor behind. You can substitute an additional 1½ cups of less-sodium chicken broth for the ale, if desired, but the flavor won't be as rich as it is with the ale.

¼ cup all-purpose flour
½ teaspoon salt
⅛ teaspoon pepper
1½ pounds lean boned round steak, cut into 1-inch cubes
Cooking spray
1 teaspoon vegetable oil
3 cups chopped onion
1½ pounds baking potato, peeled and cut into 1-inch pieces
1 pound carrots, sliced
½ teaspoon dried rosemary
½ teaspoon dried thyme
1 (14-ounce) can fat-free, less-sodium chicken broth
1 (12-ounce) bottle ale
1 tablespoon cider vinegar
1 teaspoon Worcestershire sauce
1 bay leaf

Combine flour, salt, and pepper in a shallow dish; stir well. Dredge beef in flour mixture.

Coat a Dutch oven with cooking spray; add oil, and place pan over medium-high heat until hot. Add meat and any remaining flour mixture; cook 6 minutes or until meat is browned, stirring occasionally.

Add onion, potato, and carrot to meat mixture; cook 2 minutes, stirring constantly. Stir in rosemary and remaining ingredients; bring to a boil. Cover, reduce heat, and simmer 1½ hours. Discard bay leaf. **Yield:** 5 (2-cup) servings.

Per Serving:

Calories 406	Fiber 5.6g
Fat 8.0g (sat 2.7g)	Cholesterol 79mg
Protein 35.0g	Sodium 750mg
Carbohydrate 45.0g	Exchanges 2 Starch, 3 Vegetable, 3 Lean Meat

Old-Fashioned Chicken-and-Rice Soup

Cold Cure:

There is some scientific evidence showing that the hot water vapor you inhale when you eat chicken soup helps clear your sinuses when you have a cold or the flu.

1	cup water
1	(32-ounce) carton fat-free, less-sodium chicken broth
3	(6-ounce) skinless, bone-in chicken breast halves
4	parsley sprigs
2	celery stalks, halved
1	tablespoon olive oil
1 1/3	cups chopped onion
1/2	cup chopped celery
3	carrots, halved lengthwise and sliced
2	garlic cloves, minced
1/3	cup uncooked long-grain rice
1/3	cup sliced green onions
3/4	teaspoon salt
1/2	teaspoon dried basil
1/2	teaspoon freshly ground black pepper

Combine first 5 ingredients in a Dutch oven; bring to a boil. Cover, reduce heat, and simmer 40 minutes or until chicken is tender. Remove chicken from cooking liquid; cool. Remove meat from bones, and chop. Strain broth through a sieve into a large bowl, reserving 4 1/2 cups. Reserve remaining broth for another use.

Heat oil in pan over medium-high heat. Add onion and next 3 ingredients; sauté 10 minutes or until tender. Stir in chicken, reserved broth, rice, and remaining ingredients; bring to a boil. Cover, reduce heat, and simmer 20 minutes or until rice is tender. **Yield:** 5 (1 1/2-cup) servings.

Per Serving:

Calories 205	Fiber 2.3g
Fat 4.7g (sat 0.9g)	Cholesterol 44mg
Protein 20.6g	Sodium 854mg
Carbohydrate 19.5g	Exchanges 1 Starch, 1 Vegetable, 2 Lean Meat

Prep: 10 minutes   Cook: 45 minutes

Chicken-Corn Chowder

4	bacon slices
1	cup chopped onion
1	cup diced carrot
2	garlic cloves, minced
2	cups diced peeled red potato
1	(10-ounce) package roasted chicken breast halves, skin removed, boned and diced
½	teaspoon salt
½	teaspoon black pepper
4¼	cups 2% reduced-fat milk, divided
¼	cup all-purpose flour
2	cups frozen whole-kernel corn
1½	cups (6 ounces) shredded reduced-fat sharp Cheddar cheese, divided

Simple Substitution: If you already have some cooked chicken on hand, use about 2 cups in this soup. Or you can use a 9-ounce package of frozen diced cooked chicken.

Cook bacon in a Dutch oven over medium-high heat until crisp. Remove from pan; crumble and set aside. Add onion, carrot, and garlic to pan; sauté 5 minutes. Add potato, chicken, salt, pepper, and 4 cups milk; bring to a boil. Cover, reduce heat to medium, and simmer 20 minutes or until potatoes are tender, stirring occasionally.

Place flour in a small bowl; gradually add remaining ¼ cup milk, stirring until smooth. Add flour mixture to chicken mixture. Bring to a boil over medium-high heat. Reduce heat, and simmer, uncovered, 5 minutes, stirring frequently.

Add corn and 1 cup shredded cheese to chicken mixture; stir until cheese melts. Divide mixture evenly among 9 bowls; top with crumbled bacon and remaining ½ cup shredded cheese. **Yield:** 9 (1-cup) servings.

Per Serving:

Calories 306	Fiber 2.3g
Fat 13.0g (sat 6.0g)	Cholesterol 56mg
Protein 22.5g	Sodium 567mg
Carbohydrate 25.4g	Exchanges 1½ Starch, ½ Low-Fat Milk, 2 Medium-Fat Meat

Prep: 5 minutes   Cook: 20 minutes

Dump-and-Stir Chili

Crowd Pleaser:

This quick and easy chili is a convenient and hearty dish to serve when friends drop in. Offer a variety of toppings such as fat-free sour cream, shredded Cheddar cheese, and chopped green onions.

2   (15-ounce) cans 99%-fat-free turkey chili without beans
2   (15-ounce) cans no-salt-added pinto beans, undrained
2   (14½-ounce) cans no-salt-added diced tomatoes, undrained
1   (10-ounce) can diced tomatoes and green chiles, undrained
3   tablespoons instant minced onion
1   tablespoon chili powder

Combine all ingredients in a large Dutch oven, and bring to a boil. Cover, reduce heat, and simmer 10 minutes.

Uncover and simmer 10 minutes, stirring occasionally. **Yield:** 11 (1-cup) servings.

Per Serving:

Calories 170	Fiber 7.3g
Fat 1.2g (sat 0.4g)	Cholesterol 0mg
Protein 14.1g	Sodium 591mg
Carbohydrate 25.6g	Exchanges 1½ Starch, ½ Vegetable, 1 Very Lean Meat

Prep: 20 minutes   Cook: 1 hour 20 minutes

Shrimp Gumbo

4	bacon slices
2	tablespoons vegetable oil
½	cup all-purpose flour
2	cups chopped onion
1⅔	cups chopped green bell pepper
5	garlic cloves, minced
2	cups hot water
1	cup frozen cut okra, thawed
1	(14½-ounce) can diced tomatoes, undrained
1	tablespoon Cajun seasoning
2	(8-ounce) bottles clam juice
1¼	pounds medium shrimp, peeled and deveined
1	(8-ounce) container standard oysters, undrained
1½	to 3 teaspoons hot sauce
5	cups hot cooked long-grain rice

How Shrimp Stacks Up: Shrimp is a little higher in sodium and cholesterol than other types of seafood—a 3-ounce serving has 166 grams of cholesterol and 191 milligrams of sodium—but it's still a terrific protein source with only 1 gram of fat per serving.

Cook bacon in a Dutch oven over medium heat until crisp. Remove from pan, reserving 3 tablespoons drippings in pan; crumble bacon. Add oil to drippings; place over medium heat. Add flour; cook, stirring constantly, 10 minutes or until very brown. Add onion, bell pepper, and garlic; reduce heat to medium-low, and cook, stirring constantly, 4 minutes. Add water. Add okra and next 3 ingredients. Bring to a boil; reduce heat, and simmer, uncovered, 45 minutes, stirring occasionally. **Add** shrimp and oysters; cook 10 minutes. Stir in hot sauce. Spoon rice into bowls; add gumbo. Sprinkle with crumbled bacon. **Yield:** 10 servings (serving size: ½ cup rice and 1 cup gumbo).

Per Serving:

Calories 306	Fiber 2.1g
Fat 9.8g (sat 2.9g)	Cholesterol 88mg
Protein 17.4g	Sodium 890mg
Carbohydrate 38.0g	Exchanges 2½ Starch, 1½ Very Lean Meat, 1½ Fat

Prep: 14 minutes   Cook: 6 minutes

Grilled Cheese Sandwiches Deluxe

1   cup 1% low-fat cottage cheese
½   cup (2 ounces) shredded reduced-fat sharp Cheddar cheese
4   lower-sodium bacon slices, cooked and crumbled
½   cup chopped green onions
1   tablespoon reduced-fat mayonnaise
2   teaspoons Dijon mustard
8   (½-inch) slices sourdough bread
12   (¼-inch) slices plum tomato (about 2 tomatoes)
Butter-flavored cooking spray

Calcium Counts:
This sandwich provides 279 milligrams of calcium. If you are over 50 years of age, that is 23 percent of your daily requirement.

Place cottage cheese in an electric blender; process 30 seconds or until smooth. Transfer to a small bowl; stir in Cheddar cheese and next 4 ingredients.

Spread cottage cheese mixture evenly over 4 bread slices; arrange tomato slices evenly over cottage cheese mixture. Top with remaining bread slices.

Coat a large nonstick skillet or griddle with cooking spray; place over medium heat until hot. Add sandwiches; spray each side with cooking spray, and cook 2 to 3 minutes on each side or until golden. Serve with Fresh Tomato Soup (page 146), if desired. **Yield:** 4 servings.

Per Serving:

Calories 421	**Fiber** 2.3g
Fat 10.3g (sat 3.4g)	**Cholesterol** 21mg
Protein 24.2g	**Sodium** 1,177mg
Carbohydrate 58.4g	**Exchanges** 3 Starch, 1 Low-Fat Milk, 1 Medium-Fat Meat

(Recipe for Fresh Tomato Soup on page 146)

Prep: 9 minutes   Cook: 8 minutes

Canadian BLTs

8	Canadian bacon slices
1/3	cup low-fat sour cream
1	tablespoon fat-free Italian dressing
8	(1-ounce) slices rye bread, toasted
4	romaine lettuce leaves
8	(1/4-inch-thick) slices tomato

Freshly ground black pepper

Cook bacon in a nonstick skillet over medium heat 4 minutes or until lightly browned. Remove from pan, and drain.

Stir together sour cream and Italian dressing in a small bowl. Spread evenly on one side of each bread slice.

Layer bacon, lettuce, and tomato evenly on 4 bread slices. Season with pepper. Top with remaining bread slices. **Yield:** 4 servings.

Per Serving:

Calories 276	**Fiber** 4.2g
Fat 7.1g (sat 2.3g)	**Cholesterol** 32mg
Protein 17.9g	**Sodium** 1,226mg
Carbohydrate 33.9g	**Exchanges** 2 Starch, 1 Vegetable, 1½ Medium-Fat Meat

Prep: 10 minutes

Dagwood Sandwich

3	tablespoons fat-free mayonnaise
4	(2½-ounce) submarine rolls
2	tablespoons spicy hot mustard
8	small green leaf lettuce leaves
4	(1-ounce) slices smoked turkey breast, cut in half diagonally
4	(¾-ounce) slices fat-free Swiss cheese, cut in half diagonally
4	slices small red onion
4	(1-ounce) slices turkey ham, cut in half diagonally
4	(¾-ounce) slices fat-free sharp Cheddar cheese, cut in half diagonally
4	gherkins

Spread mayonnaise evenly on top half of each roll. Spread mustard evenly on bottom half of each roll. Place 1 lettuce leaf on bottom of each roll; top each with 2 half slices of smoked turkey. Top evenly with Swiss cheese, onion, remaining lettuce leaves, turkey ham, and Cheddar cheese. Place tops of rolls on cheese.

Secure 1 gherkin on top of each sandwich with a wooden pick. **Yield:** 4 servings.

Per Serving:

Calories 326	Fiber 2.5g
Fat 4.6g (sat 1.5g)	Cholesterol 24mg
Protein 24.9g	Sodium 1,688mg
Carbohydrate 50.5g	Exchanges 3 Starch, 1 Vegetable, 2 Very Lean Meat

What's In a Name?: Named after Dagwood Bumstead, a character in the "Blondie" comic strip, this thick sandwich is piled high with a variety of meats and cheeses. Because of the deli meats, cheese, and pickles, it's higher in sodium than some of the other sandwiches in this chapter. If you need to reduce the sodium, leave off the pickles and use reduced-sodium ham and cheese.

Prep: 18 minutes

Tuna Salad Sandwiches

Simple

Substitution:

If you don't have a jar of roasted red bell peppers, you can use a 2-ounce jar of drained pimiento in this quick and easy sandwich.

2	(6-ounce) cans chunk white tuna in water, drained and flaked
¾	cup diced celery
½	cup minced onion
⅓	cup light mayonnaise
2	tablespoons minced fresh parsley
2	tablespoons drained and chopped roasted red bell pepper
2	tablespoons lemon juice
⅛	teaspoon ground white pepper
8	(1-ounce) slices whole wheat bread
8	romaine lettuce leaves

Combine first 8 ingredients in a medium bowl; stir well.

Spread tuna mixture evenly on 4 bread slices. Top each with 2 lettuce leaves and remaining bread slices. **Yield:** 4 servings.

Per Serving:

Calories 283	**Fiber** 3.6g
Fat 9.1g (sat 1.6g)	**Cholesterol** 30mg
Protein 20.6g	**Sodium** 664mg
Carbohydrate 29.9g	**Exchanges** 2 Starch, 2 Lean Meat, ½ Fat

Prep: 15 minutes   Cook: 4½ minutes

Smoked Chicken Club Sandwiches

12 (1-ounce) slices whole wheat bread, toasted
¼ cup light mayonnaise
½ pound thinly sliced smoked chicken breast
8 leaf lettuce leaves
8 thin slices tomato
4 reduced-fat bacon slices, cooked

Spread one side of each bread slice with mayonnaise. Top 4 bread slices evenly with chicken and 4 lettuce leaves; cover each with another bread slice. Top each evenly with remaining lettuce leaves, tomato slices, and bacon; cover with remaining bread slices, mayonnaise side down. Cut each sandwich into 4 triangles, and secure each triangle with a wooden pick. **Yield:** 4 servings (serving size: 4 triangles).

Microwave Shortcut: *To cook bacon in the microwave, place the slices on a microwave-safe bacon rack and cover with paper towels. Microwave at HIGH 3½ to 4½ minutes or until crisp. A general guideline for cooking bacon is about 1 minute per slice.*

Per Serving:

Calories 357	Fiber 6.7g
Fat 12.2g (sat 3.1g)	Cholesterol 41mg
Protein 21.6g	Sodium 1,205mg
Carbohydrate 47.0g	Exchanges 3 Starch, 2 Lean Meat, 1 Fat

(Photograph on page 145)

Prep: 12 minutes   Cook: 10 minutes

Classic Hamburgers

Fast Food:
Instead of going
to the local
fast-food burger
joint, grill these
lower-fat burgers
and serve them
with Cheese Fries
(page 137).

1   pound ground round
½   cup quick-cooking oats
¼   cup minced fresh parsley
1   tablespoon Dijon mustard
1   tablespoon Worcestershire sauce
½   teaspoon freshly ground black pepper
2   garlic cloves, minced
1   small onion, minced (about ¾ cup)
1   large egg white
Cooking spray
4   lettuce leaves
4   whole wheat kaiser rolls, split
8   thin slices tomato
4   slices red onion, separated into rings

Prepare grill.

Combine first 9 ingredients in a large bowl. Shape into 4 (¼-inch-thick) patties.

Place meat on grill rack coated with cooking spray; cover and grill 5 minutes on each side or until done.

Place 1 lettuce leaf on bottom half of each roll; place patties on rolls. Top each patty with 2 tomato slices, 1 onion slice, and top half of roll. **Yield:** 4 servings.

Per Serving:

Calories 383	Fiber 4.2g
Fat 10.5g (sat 3.2g)	Cholesterol 83mg
Protein 33.2g	Sodium 531mg
Carbohydrate 38.4g	Exchanges 2 Starch, 1½ Vegetable, 3½ Lean Meat

Prep: 5 minutes   Cook: 12 minutes

Saucy Dogs

½   pound ground round
1   cup chopped onion
1   (15-ounce) can sloppy joe sauce
8   low-fat frankfurters
8   hot dog buns

Combine beef and onion in a medium nonstick skillet over medium-high heat. Cook until beef is browned and onion is tender, stirring until meat crumbles. Drain, if necessary, and return to pan.

Add sloppy joe sauce to beef mixture, and bring to a boil. Reduce heat, and simmer 5 minutes, stirring occasionally.

While sauce cooks, cook frankfurters according to package directions. Place 1 frankfurter in each bun. Spoon beef mixture evenly over frankfurters. **Yield:** 8 servings.

Per Serving:

Calories 278	Fiber 0.9g
Fat 6.6g (sat 1.7g)	Cholesterol 47mg
Protein 15.4g	Sodium 806mg
Carbohydrate 36.2g	Exchanges 2 Starch, 1 Vegetable, 1 Medium-Fat Meat

CLASSIC CASSEROLES

Cheesy Potato Casserole, page 166

Cheesy Potato Casserole · Breakfast Casserole · Macaroni Casserole
Vegetable Lasagna · Vegetable Strata · Spaghetti Casserole
Extra-Easy Lasagna · Enchilada Casserole · Spanish Rice Casserole
Beefy Pot Pie · Sausage and Noodle Casserole · Chicken Casserole
Chicken Tetrazzini · Southwestern Chicken Casserole
Seafood-Artichoke Casserole

Cheesy Potato Casserole

Covered Dish

Delight:

Take this cheesy
potato side dish to
your next potluck
supper. The crunchy
potato chips make
it a real crowd
pleaser.

1   (16-ounce) container low-fat sour cream
1   (10¾-ounce) can condensed reduced-fat, reduced-sodium
         cream of chicken soup, undiluted
3   tablespoons reduced-calorie margarine, melted
¼   teaspoon salt
¼   teaspoon pepper
1   (28-ounce) package frozen hash brown potatoes with onions
         and peppers (such as Ore-Ida Potatoes O'Brien)
1   (8-ounce) package shredded reduced-fat sharp Cheddar cheese
Cooking spray
¾   cup crushed reduced-fat potato chips with ridges

Preheat oven to 375°.

Combine first 5 ingredients in a large bowl, stirring well. Add potatoes and cheese; stir potato mixture well.

Spoon potato mixture into a 13 x 9-inch baking dish coated with cooking spray. Top with potato chips. Bake, uncovered, at 375° for 1 hour or until thoroughly heated and lightly browned. **Yield:** 12 (⅔-cup) servings.

Per Serving:

Calories 140	Fiber 1.5g
Fat 7.6g (sat 4.0g)	Cholesterol 16mg
Protein 2.4g	Sodium 216mg
Carbohydrate 16.4g	Exchanges 1 Starch, 1½ Fat

(Photograph on page 165)

Breakfast Casserole

Cooking spray
1   pound 50%-less-fat sausage
1   cup fat-free milk
2   (8-ounce) cartons egg substitute
½   cup (2 ounces) shredded reduced-fat sharp Cheddar cheese
3   green onions, chopped
¾   teaspoon dry mustard
¼   teaspoon salt
¼   teaspoon ground red pepper
6   (1-ounce) slices white bread, cut into ½-inch cubes

Sausage Substitutes: The 50%-less-fat sausage has half the fat of regular pork sausage, but about the same amount of sodium. To reduce fat even more, use ground turkey sausage.

Coat a large nonstick skillet with cooking spray, and place over medium-high heat until hot. Add sausage; cook over medium heat until meat is browned, stirring to crumble. Drain and pat dry with paper towels. Set aside.

Combine milk and next 6 ingredients in a large bowl; stir well. Add sausage and bread cubes, stirring just until well blended. Pour mixture into an 11 x 7-inch baking dish coated with cooking spray. Cover and refrigerate at least 8 hours.

Preheat oven to 350°.

Bake, uncovered, at 350° for 50 minutes or until set and lightly browned. Let stand 10 minutes before serving. **Yield:** 6 servings (serving size: about 1⅓ cups).

Per Serving:

Calories 332	Fiber 0.4g
Fat 17.0g (sat 6.4g)	Cholesterol 61mg
Protein 26.2g	Sodium 964mg
Carbohydrate 16.4g	Exchanges 1 Starch, 3 Medium-Fat Meat

Prep: 10 minutes   Cook: 45 minutes

Macaroni Casserole

1   (8-ounce) package elbow macaroni
2   cups 1% low-fat cottage cheese
¼   cup fat-free milk
2   tablespoons minced fresh parsley
1   tablespoon minced fresh oregano
¼   teaspoon salt
½   teaspoon pepper
Cooking spray
½   cup (2 ounces) shredded reduced-fat Cheddar cheese
1   (8-ounce) can no-salt-added tomato sauce
¼   cup dry breadcrumbs
2   tablespoons freshly grated Parmesan cheese
Cherry tomato slices (optional)
Oregano sprigs (optional)

Pasta Pick:
Use any other variety of short pasta in this recipe. Fusilli, penne, rigatoni, rotini, seashell, and ziti are all good choices.

Cook macaroni according to package directions, omitting salt and fat. Drain.

Preheat oven to 375°.

Place cottage cheese and milk in a blender; process until smooth. Transfer to a bowl; stir in parsley and next 3 ingredients. Add macaroni, and toss. Spoon half of macaroni mixture into a 1½-quart baking dish coated with cooking spray. Sprinkle with half of Cheddar cheese; top with half of tomato sauce. Repeat layers. Sprinkle with breadcrumbs and Parmesan cheese. Bake at 375° for 30 minutes. Garnish with tomato slices and oregano, if desired. **Yield:** 4 (1¾-cup) servings.

Per Serving:

Calories 256	Fiber 1.9g
Fat 3.7g (sat 2.1g)	Cholesterol 11mg
Protein 23.3g	Sodium 978mg
Carbohydrate 30.1g	Exchanges 2 Starch, 2 Lean Meat

Prep: 10 minutes   Cook: 1 hour 15 minutes   Stand: 15 minutes

Vegetable Lasagna

*Squash
Substitution:
Use all zucchini, all
yellow squash, or a
mixture of the two.*

8   uncooked lasagna noodles
2   cups broccoli florets
2   cups thinly sliced zucchini or yellow squash
1   cup thinly sliced carrot
Cooking spray
1½ cups thinly sliced mushrooms
1   cup chopped onion
1   (16-ounce) carton 1% low-fat cottage cheese
½   cup egg substitute
3   cups spaghetti sauce
1   cup (4 ounces) shredded part-skim mozzarella cheese

Cook noodles according to package directions, omitting salt and fat. Drain.

Steam broccoli, zucchini, and carrot 5 minutes or until crisp-tender; drain, and set aside. Coat a nonstick skillet with cooking spray. Place over medium-high heat until hot. Add mushrooms and onion; sauté until tender. Add to broccoli mixture.

Preheat oven to 350°.

Combine cottage cheese and egg substitute. Spread ½ cup spaghetti sauce over bottom of a 13 x 9-inch baking dish coated with cooking spray. Place 4 lasagna noodles over sauce; top with vegetable mixture. Spoon cheese mixture over vegetables. Top with remaining 4 noodles and spaghetti sauce. Cover and bake at 350° for 40 minutes. Uncover; sprinkle with mozzarella. Bake, uncovered, 10 minutes. Let stand 15 minutes. **Yield:** 8 servings (serving size: 1 [3¼ x 4½-inch] piece).

Per Serving:

Calories 279	**Fiber** 5.0g
Fat 8.5g (sat 3.1g)	**Cholesterol** 11mg
Protein 18.2g	**Sodium** 839mg
Carbohydrate 32.7g	**Exchanges** 2 Starch, 2 Lean Meat

Prep: 15 minutes   Chill: 8 hours   Stand: 30 minutes   Cook: 40 minutes

Vegetable Strata

*Perfect Breakfast
Make Ahead: This
hearty dish is great
for breakfast or
brunch. Make it
ahead and freeze
it in an airtight
container up to 1
month. To prepare,
thaw in refrigerator
overnight and bake
according to the
recipe directions.*

1½ cups chopped fresh broccoli
4   (1-ounce) slices white bread, cubed
Butter-flavored cooking spray
1   cup (4 ounces) shredded reduced-fat Swiss cheese
¼   cup shredded carrot
2   tablespoons chopped red bell pepper
2   tablespoons chopped green onions
1½ cups 1% low-fat milk
1   cup egg substitute
½   teaspoon dry mustard
½   teaspoon hot sauce
½   teaspoon low-sodium Worcestershire sauce
¼   teaspoon pepper
⅛   teaspoon salt

Steam broccoli, covered, 3 minutes or until crisp-tender. Set aside.
Place bread cubes in a 2-quart baking dish coated with cooking spray;
sprinkle with cheese. Top with broccoli, carrot, bell pepper, and green
onions. Combine milk and remaining 6 ingredients, stirring well; pour
over broccoli mixture. Cover and chill at least 8 hours.
Remove from refrigerator, and let stand, covered, at room temperature
30 minutes.
Preheat oven to 350°.
Bake, uncovered, at 350° for 40 to 45 minutes or until set. Let stand 10
minutes before serving. **Yield:** 4 servings (serving size: about 2 cups).

Per Serving:

Calories 279	Fiber 2.1g
Fat 7.8g (sat 4.8g)	Cholesterol 24mg
Protein 21.8g	Sodium 297mg
Carbohydrate 30.1g	Exchanges 2 Starch, 2 Lean Meat

Prep: 15 minutes   Cook: 1 hour 40 minutes

Spaghetti Casserole

Freezer Fare:

*If you're cooking for
a crowd, get ahead
by making and
freezing this hearty
casserole. You can
freeze it in an
airtight container
up to 1 month.
To prepare, thaw
in refrigerator
overnight and bake
according to the
recipe directions.*

1½ pounds ground round
1½ cups chopped onion
1   cup chopped green bell pepper
½   cup chopped celery
2   garlic cloves, crushed
1   (10¾-ounce) can condensed reduced-fat, reduced-sodium
     cream of mushroom soup, undiluted
¾   cup water
1   (14.5-ounce) can diced tomatoes, undrained
2   tablespoons chili powder
¼   teaspoon pepper
1   (8-ounce) package spaghetti
1   cup (4 ounces) shredded reduced-fat Cheddar cheese, divided
2   tablespoons chopped pimiento-stuffed olives
Cooking spray

Cook first 5 ingredients in a Dutch oven over medium-high heat until
meat is browned, stirring to crumble; drain and return to pan.
Stir in soup and next 4 ingredients. Bring mixture to a boil over medium
heat. Cover, reduce heat, and simmer 1 hour, stirring occasionally.
Preheat oven to 325°.
Cook spaghetti according to package directions, omitting salt and fat.
Stir spaghetti, ½ cup cheese, and olives into meat sauce. Spoon into a
13 x 9-inch baking dish coated with cooking spray. Cover and bake at
325° for 20 minutes. Sprinkle with remaining ½ cup cheese. Bake,
uncovered, 10 minutes. **Yield:** 8 (1½-cup) servings.

Per Serving:

Calories 333	Fiber 3.1g
Fat 9.7g (sat 3.9g)	Cholesterol 62mg
Protein 29.1g	Sodium 415mg
Carbohydrate 32.0g	Exchanges 2 Starch, 3 Lean Meat

Extra-Easy Lasagna

Lazy Lasagna:
This shortcut recipe lets you make hearty lasagna the easy way—with only seven ingredients and without having to boil the lasagna noodles.

1   pound ground round
1   (26-ounce) bottle tomato-basil pasta sauce
Cooking spray
6   uncooked lasagna noodles
1   (15-ounce) carton part-skim ricotta cheese
1½   cups (6 ounces) shredded part-skim mozzarella cheese
¼   cup hot water

Cook meat in a large nonstick skillet over medium heat until browned, stirring to crumble. Drain; wipe drippings from pan with paper towels. Return meat to pan. Stir in pasta sauce.
Preheat oven to 375°.
Spread one-third of meat mixture in bottom of an 11 x 7-inch baking dish coated with cooking spray. Arrange 3 noodles over meat mixture; top with half of ricotta cheese and half of mozzarella cheese. Repeat layers, ending with last one-third of meat mixture. Slowly pour water into dish. Tightly cover baking dish with heavy-duty foil.
Bake at 375° for 45 minutes. Uncover and bake an additional 10 minutes. Let stand 10 minutes before serving. **Yield:** 6 servings (serving size: about 1⅓ cups).

Per Serving:

Calories 406	Fiber 1.8g
Fat 15.2g (sat 8.1g)	Cholesterol 81mg
Protein 36.4g	Sodium 650mg
Carbohydrate 29.1g	Exchanges 2 Starch, 4 Lean Meat

Prep: 5 minutes   Cook: 25 minutes

Enchilada Casserole

2   pounds ground round
1   cup chopped onion
2   (8-ounce) cans no-salt-added tomato sauce
1   (11-ounce) can Mexicorn, drained
1   (10-ounce) can enchilada sauce
1   teaspoon chili powder
½   teaspoon dried oregano
½   teaspoon pepper
1   (6½-ounce) package corn tortillas, divided
Cooking spray
2   cups (8 ounces) shredded reduced-fat Cheddar cheese, divided
Green chile peppers (optional)

Reduce Your Risk: Canned tomato products such as tomato sauce are high in lycopene, which has been shown to help reduce the risk of prostate cancer.

Cook beef and onion in a large nonstick skillet over medium-high heat until browned, stirring to crumble. Drain.

Stir tomato sauce and next 5 ingredients into meat mixture; bring to a boil. Reduce heat to medium, and cook, uncovered, 5 minutes, stirring occasionally.

Preheat oven to 375°.

Place half of tortillas in bottom of a 13 x 9-inch baking dish coated with cooking spray. Spoon half of beef mixture over tortillas; sprinkle with 1 cup cheese. Repeat layers with remaining tortillas and beef mixture. Bake at 375° for 10 minutes. Sprinkle with remaining cheese; bake 5 minutes or until cheese melts. Garnish with chile peppers, if desired.

Yield: 8 servings (serving size: about 1¾ cups).

Per Serving:

Calories 357	Fiber 3.3g
Fat 13.4g (sat 5.4g)	Cholesterol 47mg
Protein 32.7g	Sodium 735mg
Carbohydrate 24.8g	Exchanges 1 Starch, 2 Vegetable, 4 Lean Meat

Spanish Rice Casserole

Quick Rice:

When a recipe calls for cooked rice, use boil-in-bag rice. It only takes about 10 minutes to cook, and one regular-size bag gives you 2 cups cooked rice.

1	pound ground round
1	cup chopped green bell pepper
2	cups chopped onion
1	(4-ounce) can sliced mushrooms, drained
2	(8-ounce) cans no-salt-added tomato sauce
2	packets calorie-free sweetener
1/8	teaspoon salt
1/4	cup picante sauce
2	cups cooked long-grain rice
1/2	cup (2 ounces) shredded reduced-fat sharp Cheddar cheese

Cook beef, bell pepper, onion, and mushrooms in a large nonstick skillet over medium-high heat until beef is browned, stirring to crumble; drain.

Stir in tomato sauce and next 4 ingredients. Cook over medium heat until thoroughly heated. Sprinkle with cheese; cook 5 minutes or until cheese melts. **Yield:** 4 (1¾-cup) servings.

Per Serving:

Calories 420	Fiber 4.2g
Fat 13.8g (sat 6.2g)	Cholesterol 51mg
Protein 32.0g	Sodium 487mg
Carbohydrate 40.4g	Exchanges 2 Starch, 2 Vegetable, 3 Medium-Fat Meat

Prep: 10 minutes   Cook: 43 minutes

Beefy Pot Pie

1½ pounds ground round
1   (1.61-ounce) envelope no-fat brown gravy mix
      (such as Pioneer Brand)
1½ cups water
2   (15-ounce) cans mixed vegetables, drained
1   (10¾-ounce) can condensed reduced-fat, reduced-sodium
      cream of mushroom soup, undiluted
¼   teaspoon pepper
1½ cups low-fat baking mix (such as reduced-fat Bisquick)
¾   cup fat-free milk
Butter-flavored cooking spray
1   cup (4 ounces) shredded reduced-fat Cheddar cheese

Sodium Solution: Because of the convenience products in this recipe (canned vegetables, soup, gravy mix, and biscuit mix), it's high in sodium. If you need to reduce the sodium slightly, use about 2 cups frozen mixed vegetables instead of canned.

Preheat oven to 400°.

Cook beef in a nonstick skillet over medium heat until browned, stirring to crumble. Drain and pat dry with paper towels. Wipe drippings from pan with a paper towel. Return beef to pan. Set aside.

Combine gravy mix and water; stir until smooth. Add to beef in pan. Add vegetables, soup, and pepper; bring to a boil. Reduce heat, and simmer, uncovered, 5 minutes.

Combine baking mix and milk; stir until smooth. Spoon beef mixture into a 13 x 9-inch baking dish coated with cooking spray. Top with cheese. Spread biscuit mixture over beef mixture (biscuit mixture will be a thin layer over beef mixture). Coat top of biscuit mixture with cooking spray. Bake, uncovered, at 400° for 25 minutes or until top is golden. **Yield:** 8 (1-cup) servings.

Per Serving:

Calories 324	Fiber 2.4g
Fat 9.6g (sat 3.7g)	Cholesterol 58mg
Protein 27.1g	Sodium 1,074mg
Carbohydrate 30.4g	Exchanges 2 Starch, 3 Lean Meat

Prep: 10 minutes   Cook: 1 hour

Sausage and Noodle Casserole

Where To Find It:

Look for light bulk pork-and-turkey sausage either in the refrigerated meats/cold cuts section or the freezer case of your supermarket.

1   (8-ounce) package medium egg noodles
1   pound light bulk pork-and-turkey sausage
1   (10¾-ounce) can condensed reduced-fat, reduced-sodium cream of chicken soup, undiluted
1   (8-ounce) carton fat-free sour cream
⅓   cup crumbled blue cheese
1   (4½-ounce) jar sliced mushrooms, drained
1   (2-ounce) jar diced pimiento, drained
2   tablespoons finely chopped green bell pepper
Cooking spray
½   cup soft breadcrumbs
2   teaspoons reduced-calorie margarine, melted

Cook noodles according to package directions, omitting salt and fat; drain and set aside.

Preheat oven to 350°.

Cook sausage in a large nonstick skillet over medium-high heat until browned, stirring to crumble; drain and set aside.

Combine soup, sour cream, and blue cheese in a large saucepan; cook over medium heat, stirring constantly, until cheese melts. Add noodles, sausage, mushrooms, pimiento, and bell pepper, tossing to coat. Spoon into an 11 x 7-inch baking dish coated with cooking spray.

Combine breadcrumbs and margarine; sprinkle over casserole. Bake, uncovered, at 350° for 30 minutes. **Yield:** 6 servings (serving size: about 1⅓ cups).

Per Serving:

Calories 327	Fiber 1.6g
Fat 8.2g (sat 3.4g)	Cholesterol 69mg
Protein 21.4g	Sodium 952mg
Carbohydrate 42.4g	Exchanges 3 Starch, 2 Lean Meat

Prep: 15 minutes   Cook: 40 minutes

Chicken Casserole

3   cups chopped cooked chicken breast
1½   cups cooked long-grain rice
2   hard-cooked large eggs, chopped
1   (10¾-ounce) can condensed reduced-fat, reduced-sodium
        cream of mushroom soup, undiluted
¾   cup chopped celery
1½   tablespoons chopped onion
⅓   cup light mayonnaise
1   tablespoon fresh lemon juice
¼   teaspoon pepper
Cooking spray
24   reduced-fat round buttery crackers, coarsely crushed
1   tablespoon margarine

Quick Chicken:
If you don't have
leftover chicken
on hand, use
deli-roasted
chicken, a package
of cooked chicken
strips, or frozen
diced cooked
chicken.

Preheat oven to 350°.
Combine first 9 ingredients; mix well. Spoon into an 11 x 7-inch baking dish coated with cooking spray. Stir together crushed crackers and margarine. Sprinkle over chicken mixture. Bake at 350° for 40 minutes. **Yield:** 6 servings (serving size: about 1⅓ cups).

Per Serving:

Calories 333	Fiber 0.5g
Fat 12.8g (sat 2.7g)	Cholesterol 145mg
Protein 25.3g	Sodium 520mg
Carbohydrate 26.4g	Exchanges 1½ Starch, 3 Lean Meat, 1 Fat

Prep: 12 minutes   Cook: 25 minutes

Chicken Tetrazzini

Timesaving Tip:
Keep preparation
time to a minimum
by using rotisserie
chicken, presliced
mushrooms, and
frozen chopped
onion and pepper.

8   ounces uncooked spaghetti
1   (14-ounce) can fat-free, less-sodium chicken broth
½   (8-ounce) package sliced mushrooms
½   cup chopped green bell pepper
⅓   cup chopped onion
1   cup fat-free evaporated milk
⅓   cup all-purpose flour
¼   teaspoon black pepper
⅛   teaspoon ground nutmeg
2   cups chopped cooked chicken breast
2   tablespoons dry sherry or fat-free evaporated milk
Cooking spray
¼   cup (1 ounce) freshly grated Parmesan cheese

Cook spaghetti according to package directions, omitting salt and fat. Drain and set aside.

Preheat oven to 400°.

Combine broth and next 3 ingredients in a large saucepan. Bring to a boil; cover, reduce heat, and simmer 5 minutes or until vegetables are tender. Combine evaporated milk and next 3 ingredients, stirring well with a whisk. Add to vegetable mixture. Cook over medium heat until mixture is thick and bubbly, stirring constantly. Add chicken and sherry.

Toss cooked spaghetti with chicken mixture. Spoon into an 8-inch square baking dish coated with cooking spray. Sprinkle with Parmesan cheese. Bake, uncovered, at 400° for 10 minutes or until golden.

Yield: 6 (1-cup) servings.

Per Serving:

Calories 315

Fat 3.7g (sat 1.3g)

Protein 26.5g

Carbohydrate 41.3g

Fiber 1.7g

Cholesterol 48mg

Sodium 305mg

Exchanges 3 Starch, 2½ Very Lean Meat

Prep: 15 minutes   Cook: 42 minutes   Stand: 5 minutes

Southwestern Chicken Casserole

¾   cup chopped green bell pepper
1½   cups chopped onion
Cooking spray
3   cups frozen cooked diced chicken breast, thawed
       (about 1 pound)
1   (10-ounce) can diced tomatoes and green chiles
1   (14-ounce) can no-salt-added diced tomatoes
1   (10¾-ounce) can condensed reduced-fat, reduced-sodium
       cream of chicken soup, undiluted
1   (10¾-ounce) can condensed reduced-fat, reduced-sodium
       cream of mushroom soup, undiluted
12   (6-inch) corn tortillas, cut into quarters
1½   cups (6 ounces) shredded reduced-fat sharp Cheddar cheese

Simple Substitution: If you want to use fresh cooked chicken, you'll need to start with about 1 pound of uncooked chicken breasts to get 3 cups cooked.

Preheat oven to 325°.

Place a large nonstick skillet over medium-high heat until hot. Coat bell pepper and onion with cooking spray; add to pan. Sauté 4 minutes or until tender. Add chicken and cook until thoroughly heated. Remove from heat; stir in tomatoes and soups.

Place one-third of tortillas in a 13 x 9-inch baking dish coated with cooking spray. Top with one-third of chicken mixture; sprinkle with ⅓ cup cheese. Repeat layers twice, reserving ½ cup cheese for topping.

Bake, uncovered, at 325° for 35 minutes. Sprinkle with remaining ½ cup cheese, and bake an additional 5 minutes. Let stand 5 minutes before serving. **Yield:** 8 servings (serving size: about 1½ cups).

Per Serving:

Calories 265	Fiber 3.8g
Fat 4.7g (sat 1.9g)	Cholesterol 44mg
Protein 22.7g	Sodium 673mg
Carbohydrate 33.1g	Exchanges 2 Starch, 1 Vegetable, 2 Lean Meat

Seafood-Artichoke Casserole

8	cups water
1½	pounds medium shrimp, peeled and deveined
1	(14-ounce) can artichoke hearts, drained and quartered
1	(6-ounce) can lump crabmeat, drained
¼	cup chopped celery
2	tablespoons chopped green onions
½	cup plain fat-free yogurt
½	cup fat-free mayonnaise
1	teaspoon low-sodium Worcestershire sauce
¼	teaspoon ground white pepper
	Cooking spray
3	tablespoons dry breadcrumbs
¼	teaspoon paprika

Preheat oven to 350°.

Bring water to a boil; add shrimp, and cook 3 to 5 minutes or until done. Drain well. Place shrimp in a large bowl; add artichoke hearts, crabmeat, celery, and green onions, tossing gently.

Combine yogurt and next 3 ingredients. Stir yogurt mixture into shrimp mixture; spoon into a 1-quart baking dish coated with cooking spray. Combine breadcrumbs and paprika; sprinkle over shrimp mixture. Bake at 350° for 30 minutes or until lightly browned. Serve immediately. **Yield:** 4 (1-cup) servings.

Per Serving:

Calories 215	Fiber 2.7g
Fat 1.6g (sat 0.4g)	Cholesterol 207mg
Protein 30.1g	Sodium 1,078mg
Carbohydrate 19.7g	Exchanges 1 Starch, 1 Vegetable, 3 Very Lean Meat

HOLIDAY MENUS

Spiced Pumpkin Pie, page 188

Family Thanksgiving Dinner

Begin the holiday season with this traditional turkey dinner.

Christmas Eve Feast

With this easy menu, you'll have plenty of time for family and friends.

Celebration of Lights

Serve traditional Hanukkah dishes without the excess fat and calories.

Easter Dinner

Ham steals the show with this fresh, springtime menu.

4th of July Barbecue

Celebrate Independence Day with this "freedom-from-the-kitchen" meal.

FAMILY THANKSGIVING DINNER

Serves 8
Herb-Roasted Turkey (page 185)
Turkey Gravy (page 186)
Green Beans with Lemon and Garlic (page 187)
Sweet Potato Casserole (page 140)
Corn Bread Dressing (page 186)
Cranberry-Pear Relish (page 187)
Whole wheat rolls
Spiced Pumpkin Pie (page 188)

Herb-Roasted Turkey

Herb-Roasted Turkey

Prep: 20 minutes   Cook: 3 hours, 30 minutes

1 (12-pound) turkey
8 thyme sprigs, divided
6 rosemary sprigs, divided
6 sage sprigs, divided
½ teaspoon poultry seasoning
¼ teaspoon salt
¼ teaspoon pepper
1 onion, quartered
2 celery stalks, each cut into 4 pieces
Cooking spray

Preheat oven to 325°.

Remove and discard giblets and neck from turkey. Rinse turkey with cold water; pat dry. Trim excess fat. Starting at neck cavity, loosen skin from breast and drumsticks by inserting fingers, gently pushing between skin and meat.

Arrange a thyme sprig beneath skin on each drumstick. Arrange 2 sprigs each of thyme, rosemary, and sage beneath skin on each breast half. Gently press skin to secure.

Combine poultry seasoning, salt, and pepper. Sprinkle body cavity with half of seasoning mixture. Place 2 onion quarters, 4 celery pieces, and 1 sprig each of thyme, rosemary, and sage into body cavity. Repeat procedure for neck cavity.

Lift wing tips up and over back; tuck under turkey. Place turkey, breast side up, on a rack coated with cooking spray; place rack in a shallow roasting pan. Coat turkey with cooking spray. Insert meat thermometer into meaty part of thigh, making sure not to touch bone. Cover loosely with aluminum foil; bake at 325° for 2 hours. Uncover; bake 1 hour. Bake, uncovered, 30 additional minutes or until meat thermometer registers 180°. Cover turkey loosely with aluminum foil; let stand 20 minutes. Transfer turkey to a serving platter; if desired, garnish with fresh herbs, oranges, and grapes. Carefully pour pan drippings into a four-cup measure. Degrease and reserve for Turkey Gravy recipe on page 186. **Yield:** 23 servings (serving size: about 4 ounces roasted turkey).

Per Serving: Calories 144   Fat 4.1g   (sat 1.4g)   Protein 24.9g   Carbohydrate 0.0g
Fiber 0.2g   Cholesterol 64mg   Sodium 85mg
Exchanges: 3 Very Lean Meat

How to Degrease Turkey Drippings: For a quick way to remove fat from turkey drippings, carefully pour pan drippings into a four-cup measure. Be careful. The roasting pan and drippings may still be hot. Pour the drippings in a large heavy-duty zip-top plastic bag (the fat will rise to the top). Wipe measure with a paper towel to remove any remaining fat. Carefully snip off one corner of the bag. Begin draining the drippings into the four-cup measure, stopping before the fat layer reaches the opening.

Turkey Gravy

Prep: 5 minutes   Cook: 7 minutes

1 tablespoon margarine

3 tablespoons all-purpose flour

1 cup low-sodium chicken broth

1 cup degreased turkey drippings

¼ cup dry white wine

¼ teaspoon salt

Melt margarine in a heavy saucepan over medium heat. Stir in flour, and cook 1 minute, stirring constantly with a wire whisk. Gradually add chicken broth and remaining ingredients, stirring constantly. **Bring** to a boil, stirring constantly. Reduce heat; simmer, uncovered, 5 minutes or until slightly thick. **Yield:** 7 (⅓-cup) servings.

Per Serving: Calories 57   Fat 2.8g   (sat 0.6g)   Protein 3.3g   Carbohydrate 3.2g
Fiber 0.1g   Cholesterol 6mg   Sodium 128mg
Exchange: ½ Fat

Corn Bread Dressing

Prep: 20 minutes   Cook: 1 hour

1 cup yellow cornmeal

1 teaspoon baking powder

¼ teaspoon baking soda

1 cup low-fat buttermilk (1%)

⅓ cup egg substitute

1 tablespoon vegetable oil

Cooking spray

1½ tablespoons reduced-calorie margarine

½ cup chopped celery

½ cup chopped onion

2 slices white bread, torn

2 cups fat-free, less-sodium chicken broth

1 teaspoon poultry seasoning

½ teaspoon rubbed sage

¼ teaspoon pepper

Preheat oven to 450°.

Combine first 3 ingredients; make a well in center of mixture. Combine buttermilk, egg substitute, and oil; add to cornmeal mixture and stir. Pour into an 8-inch square baking pan coated with cooking spray. Bake at 450° for 15 minutes. Remove from pan; cool.

Melt margarine in a nonstick skillet. Add celery and onion; sauté 5 minutes. Crumble corn bread. Add vegetables, bread, and remaining ingredients. Spoon into an 11 x 7-inch baking dish coated with cooking spray. Bake at 325° for 40 minutes. **Yield:** 8 (¾-cup) servings.

Per Serving: Calories 149   Fat 3.8g   (sat 0.8g)   Protein 5.2g   Carbohydrate 23.5g
Fiber 0.8g   Cholesterol 2mg   Sodium 390mg
Exchanges: 1½ Starch, ½ Fat

Green Beans with Lemon and Garlic

Prep: 10 minutes   Cook: 13 minutes

1½ cups water
2 pounds fresh green beans, trimmed
1½ tablespoons olive oil
6 garlic cloves, minced

⅓ cup fresh lemon juice
¼ teaspoon salt
¼ teaspoon pepper

Bring water to a boil in a large nonstick skillet; add beans. Cook 5 minutes; drain. Set beans aside.

Heat oil in pan over medium-high heat. Add garlic and beans; sauté 2 minutes. Add lemon juice, salt, and pepper; sauté 2 minutes. **Yield:** 8 (1-cup) servings.

Per Serving: Calories 66   Fat 2.9g   (sat 0.3g)   Protein 2.3g   Carbohydrate 9.9g
Fiber 2.5g   Cholesterol 0mg   Sodium 78mg
Exchanges: 1 Vegetable, ½ Fat

Cranberry-Pear Relish

Prep: 15 minutes   Chill: 8 hours

1½ cups fresh or frozen cranberries
¾ cup chopped peeled pear
¼ cup "measures-like-sugar" calorie-free
    sweetener
1 teaspoon grated orange rind

¼ cup chopped peeled orange
¼ cup canned crushed pineapple in
    juice, drained
¼ teaspoon ground ginger

Process cranberries in a food processor 5 seconds or until cranberries are coarsely chopped.

Transfer to a bowl. Stir in pear and next 5 ingredients. Cover and chill at least 8 hours. Serve with roasted turkey. **Yield:** 8 (¼-cup) servings.

Per Serving: Calories 28   Fat 0.1g   (sat 0.0g)   Protein 0.2g   Carbohydrate 7.1g   Fiber 1.4g
Cholesterol 0mg   Sodium 1mg
Exchange: ½ Fruit

Spiced Pumpkin Pie

Prep: 6 minutes   Chill: 4 hours

1½ cups fat-free milk

2 (1-ounce) packages vanilla sugar-free, fat-free instant pudding mix

1 (15-ounce) can mashed pumpkin

½ teaspoon vanilla extract

1 teaspoon ground cinnamon

¼ teaspoon ground ginger

⅛ teaspoon ground cloves

1 (9-ounce) graham cracker crust

Frozen fat-free whipped topping, thawed (optional)

Ground cinnamon (optional)

Combine milk and pudding mix in a medium bowl. Beat 2 minutes with a mixer at low speed (mixture will be thick).

Stir in pumpkin and next 4 ingredients. Spoon pumpkin mixture into crust. Cover and chill at least 4 hours or until firm.

Top with whipped topping and sprinkle with additional cinnamon, if desired. **Yield:** 8 servings (serving size: 1 slice).

Per Serving: Calories 206   Fat 7.5g   (sat 1.6g)   Protein 3.7g   Carbohydrate 31.8g
Fiber 2.8g   Cholesterol 1mg   Sodium 333mg
Exchanges: 2 Starch, 1 Fat

(Photograph on page 183)

CHRISTMAS EVE FEAST

Peppered Beef Tenderloin

Peppered Beef Tenderloin

Prep: 5 minutes   Chill: 24 hours
Cook: 50 minutes

1 (8-ounce) carton reduced-fat sour cream
3 tablespoons Dijon mustard
2 tablespoons prepared horseradish
2 tablespoons whole green peppercorns
2 tablespoons whole red peppercorns
2 teaspoons coarse salt
Cooking spray

1 (3½-pound) beef tenderloin, trimmed
1 cup chopped fresh flat-leaf parsley
¼ cup light butter, softened
3 tablespoons Dijon mustard
Baby artichokes (optional)
Rosemary sprigs (optional)

Combine first 3 ingredients. Cover; chill.

Place peppercorns in a blender; pulse until chopped. Transfer to a bowl, and stir in salt.

Place beef on a broiler pan coated with cooking spray. Combine parsley, butter, and 3 tablespoons mustard; rub evenly over beef. Pat peppercorn mixture evenly over beef. Cover and chill up to 24 hours.

Preheat oven to 350°.

Insert meat thermometer into thickest portion of beef. Bake at 350° for 50 minutes or until thermometer registers 145° (medium-rare) to 160° (medium). Transfer beef to a platter; cover loosely with foil. Let stand 10 minutes before slicing. Serve with sour cream mixture. If desired, garnish with artichokes and rosemary. **Yield:** 14 servings.

Per Serving: Calories 225   Fat 11.9g   (sat 5.2g)   Protein 25.7g   Carbohydrate 3.3g
Fiber 0.8g   Cholesterol 85mg   Sodium 588mg
Exchanges: 3 Medium-Fat Meat

Sweet-and-Sour Brussels Sprouts with Bacon

Prep: 5 minutes   Cook: 17 minutes

1¼ pounds Brussels sprouts, trimmed and
       halved lengthwise
3 lower-sodium bacon slices
2 tablespoons dark brown sugar

3 tablespoons white wine vinegar
½ teaspoon salt
¼ teaspoon pepper

Place Brussels sprouts in a large nonstick skillet; add water to cover. Bring to a boil; reduce heat, and simmer, uncovered, 5 minutes. Drain; cover and keep warm. Set aside.

Cook bacon in a large nonstick skillet over medium heat until crisp. Remove bacon from pan; crumble and set aside. Pour excess fat from pan, reserving any brown bits; discard fat.

Add sugar, vinegar, salt, and pepper to pan, stirring to dissolve sugar. Return Brussels sprouts to pan, and cook until thoroughly heated. Stir in reserved bacon. **Yield:** 8 (½-cup) servings.

Per Serving: Calories 50   Fat 1.5g   (sat 0.5g)   Protein 3.0g   Carbohydrate 7.7g
Fiber 2.6g   Cholesterol 3mg   Sodium 206mg
Exchanges: 2 Vegetable, ½ Fat

Dijon Scalloped Potatoes

Prep: 20 minutes   Cook: 1 hour, 10 minutes

¾ cup fat-free, less-sodium chicken broth

½ cup sliced leeks

½ cup fat-free milk

2 tablespoons all-purpose flour

1 tablespoon Dijon mustard

¼ teaspoon dried dill

¼ teaspoon salt

⅛ to ¼ teaspoon pepper

4 cups thinly sliced peeled baking potato (about 1½ pounds)

Cooking spray

Preheat oven to 350°.

Combine broth and leeks in a medium saucepan; bring to a boil. Cover, reduce heat, and simmer 5 minutes. Combine milk and next 5 ingredients, stirring with a whisk until smooth. Add to broth mixture, stirring well. Cook 3 minutes or until mixture is thick and bubbly, stirring constantly. Remove from heat.

Layer half of potato in a 1½-quart baking dish coated with cooking spray; pour half of leek mixture over potato. Repeat layers with remaining potato and leek mixture. Cover and bake at 350° for 55 minutes. Uncover and bake 15 minutes or until potato is tender and lightly browned. **Yield:** 8 (½-cup) servings.

Per Serving: Calories 87   Fat 0.4g   (sat 0.1g)   Protein 2.2g   Carbohydrate 18.8g
Fiber 1.3g   Cholesterol 0mg   Sodium 142mg
Exchange: 1 Starch

Holiday Ambrosia

2 (15¼-ounce) cans chunk pineapple in
  juice, drained
2 cups pink grapefruit sections

2 cups orange sections
½ cup coconut, toasted

Combine first 3 ingredients in a medium bowl; toss gently. Sprinkle with coconut. Cover and chill. **Yield:** 8 (¾-cup) servings.

Per Serving: Calories 112 Fat 2.2g (sat 1.8g) Protein 1.0g Carbohydrate 23.5g
Fiber 2.9g Cholesterol 0mg Sodium 16mg
Exchanges: 1½ Fruit, ½ Fat

Mixed Fruit Trifle

2 (1-ounce) packages vanilla sugar-free,
  fat-free instant pudding mix
4 cups fat-free milk
2 (3-ounce) packages cake-style
  ladyfingers (24 ladyfingers)
⅓ cup low-sugar strawberry spread, melted

2 cups halved strawberries
2 cups cubed pineapple
1 cup halved seedless green grapes
1 cup halved seedless red grapes
1 (8-ounce) container frozen fat-free
  whipped topping, thawed

Prepare pudding according to package directions, using 4 cups fat-free milk. Cover and chill.

Tear ladyfingers into bite-size pieces; place half in a 3-quart trifle bowl. Brush cake with strawberry spread.

Combine strawberries, pineapple, and grapes. Place half of fruit over cake. Top with half of pudding. Repeat procedure with remaining cake, fruit, and pudding. Top with whipped topping. Cover and chill. **Yield:** 16 servings (serving size: about ¾ cup).

Per Serving: Calories 126 Fat 0.9g (sat 0.2g) Protein 3.3g Carbohydrate 25.9g
Fiber 1.0g Cholesterol 20mg Sodium 282mg
Exchanges: 1 Starch, 1 Fruit

CELEBRATION OF LIGHTS

Simple Roast Chicken and
Sweet Potato Cakes

Simple Roast Chicken

Prep: 20 minutes   Cook: 1 hour

1 (4-pound) roasting chicken
½ teaspoon salt
½ teaspoon pepper
½ teaspoon paprika
1 onion, trimmed and quartered
1 celery stalk, cut into 3-inch pieces

1 carrot, cut into 3-inch pieces
1 garlic clove
1 bay leaf
Cooking spray
Carrot curls (optional)
Celery leaves (optional)

Preheat oven to 400°.

Remove and discard giblets and neck from chicken. Rinse chicken under cold water; pat dry. Trim fat from chicken. Combine salt, pepper, and paprika; sprinkle over chicken and into cavity. Place onion and next 4 ingredients in cavity. Tie ends of legs together with cord. Lift wing tips up and over back; tuck under chicken.

Place chicken, breast side up, on rack of a broiler pan coated with cooking spray. Insert meat thermometer into meaty part of thigh, making sure it does not touch bone. Bake at 400° for 1 hour or until meat thermometer registers 180°. Cover chicken loosely with aluminum foil; let stand 10 minutes. Before serving, remove and discard skin, vegetables, and bay leaf. If desired, garnish with carrot curls and celery leaves. **Yield:** 6 servings (serving size: about 3 ounces chicken).

Per Serving: Calories 176   Fat 6.3g   (sat 1.7g)   Protein 24.2g   Carbohydrate 4.3g
Fiber 1.0g   Cholesterol 71mg   Sodium 278mg
Exchanges: 1 Vegetable, 3 Lean Meat

Homemade Applesauce

Prep: 15 minutes   Cook: 45 minutes

5 cups coarsely chopped peeled red
    cooking apple (about 1½ pounds)
½ cup apple juice

¼ cup "measures-like-sugar" brown
    sugar calorie-free sweetener

Combine all ingredients in a large saucepan. Bring to a boil. Reduce heat; simmer 45 minutes or until apple is tender, stirring occasionally. Serve warm or chilled. **Yield:** 6 (⅔-cup) servings.

Per Serving: Calories 92   Fat 0.6g   (sat 0.1g)   Protein 0.4g   Carbohydrate 23.6g
Fiber 4.0g   Cholesterol 0mg   Sodium 7mg
Exchanges: 1½ Fruit

Sweet Potato Cakes

Prep: 10 minutes   Cook: 8 minutes per batch

4 cups shredded peeled sweet potato

¼ cup all-purpose flour

1 teaspoon instant minced onion

⅛ teaspoon salt

⅛ teaspoon pepper

Dash of ground nutmeg

1 large egg, lightly beaten

Cooking spray

Combine first 7 ingredients. Coat a nonstick skillet with cooking spray. For each cake, spoon ¼ cup mixture into pan; flatten with a spatula. Cook 4 minutes on each side or until golden. **Yield:** 12 cakes.

Per Cake: Calories 85 Fat 0.6g (sat 0.2g) Protein 2.0g Carbohydrate 18.3g
Fiber 2.1g Cholesterol 18mg Sodium 36mg
Exchange: 1 Starch

Mandel Bread

Prep: 30 minutes   Cook: 1 hour

4 large eggs

1 cup plus 3 tablespoons "measures-like-
   sugar" calorie-free sweetener, divided

⅓ cup vegetable oil

1 tablespoon grated lemon rind

1 tablespoon fresh lemon juice

¼ teaspoon almond extract

½ cup potato starch

½ cup matzo cake meal

½ teaspoon salt

½ cup chopped walnuts

Cooking spray

1½ teaspoons ground cinnamon

Preheat oven to 350°. Beat eggs and 1 cup sweetener with a mixer at high speed 2 minutes. Combine oil and next 3 ingredients; add to egg mixture, beating until fluffy. Combine potato starch, meal, and salt. Fold into egg mixture. Stir in nuts.

Pour into 2 (9 x 5-inch) loaf pans coated with cooking spray and sprinkled with flour. Bake at 350° for 25 minutes (loaves will be thin). Cool in pans on wire racks 10 minutes; remove from pans. Cool on wire racks. Combine 3 tablespoons sweetener and cinnamon; stir. Cut loaves into ½-inch-thick slices; place on an ungreased baking sheet. Sprinkle with cinnamon mixture. Bake at 325° for 35 minutes. **Yield:** 2 dozen.

Per Slice: Calories 87 Fat 5.6g (sat 0.6g) Protein 1.7g Carbohydrate 12.4g
Fiber 0.3g Cholesterol 35mg Sodium 59mg
Exchanges: 1 Starch, 1 Fat

EASTER DINNER

Serves 8

Orange-Baked Ham

Orange-Baked Ham

1 (2-pound) reduced-fat cooked ham
½ cup frozen orange juice concentrate,
    thawed
¼ cup water
3 tablespoons "measures-like-sugar" brown
    sugar calorie-free sweetener

2 teaspoons white wine vinegar
1 teaspoon dry mustard
½ teaspoon grated orange rind
¼ teaspoon ground ginger
Cooking spray
Whole cloves

Score ham in a diamond design; place in a large heavy-duty zip-top plastic bag. Combine juice concentrate and next 6 ingredients; pour over ham. Seal bag; shake until ham is well coated. Marinate in refrigerator at least 8 hours, turning occasionally.

Preheat oven to 325°.

Remove ham from marinade, and set aside ½ cup marinade. Place ham on a rack in a roasting pan coated with cooking spray; stud ham with cloves. Brush ham with reserved marinade. Cover; bake at 325° for 1½ hours, basting occasionally during first hour. Let stand 10 minutes. Remove and discard cloves. **Yield:** 16 (2-ounce) slices.

Per Serving: Calories 99   Fat 3.2g   (sat 0.9g)   Protein 12.1g   Carbohydrate 4.8g
Fiber 0.1g   Cholesterol 30mg   Sodium 685mg
Exchanges: 2 Lean Meat

Asparagus with Lemon

2 pounds asparagus
2 tablespoons light butter
¼ cup fresh lemon juice

¼ teaspoon salt
3 tablespoons preshredded fresh
    Parmesan cheese

Snap off tough ends of asparagus. Steam asparagus, covered, 5 minutes; drain. Plunge into ice water to stop the cooking process; drain.

Melt butter in a skillet over medium heat; stir in lemon juice and salt. Add asparagus, and cook just until heated; transfer to a platter. Drizzle with sauce; sprinkle with Parmesan cheese. **Yield:** 8 servings.

Per Serving: Calories 53   Fat 2.0g   (sat 1.3g)   Protein 3.4g   Carbohydrate 5.6g
Fiber 2.5g   Cholesterol 6.4mg   Sodium 122mg
Exchanges: 1 Vegetable, ½ Fat

Rosemary Biscuits

Prep: 10 minutes   Cook: 8 minutes

4 cups low-fat baking mix (such as
     reduced-fat Bisquick)
1½ teaspoons dried rosemary, crushed

1⅓ cups fat-free milk
Butter-flavored cooking spray

Preheat oven to 450°.

Combine baking mix and rosemary in a large bowl. Add milk, stirring just until moist. Turn dough out onto a lightly floured surface, and knead lightly 3 or 4 times.

Roll dough to a ½-inch thickness; cut with a 2-inch round cutter, and place on a baking sheet coated with cooking spray. Coat tops of biscuits with cooking spray.

Bake at 450° for 8 minutes or until lightly browned. **Yield:** 2½ dozen.

Per Biscuit: Calories 86   Fat 0.2g   (sat 0.0g)   Protein 2.0g   Carbohydrate 21.9g
Fiber 0.0g   Cholesterol 0mg   Sodium 278mg
Exchange: 1 Starch

Creamy Strawberry Pie

Prep: 15 minutes   Cook: 8 minutes
Chill: 10 minutes; 3 hours

½ (15-ounce) package refrigerated piecrusts
1 (0.3-ounce) package strawberry-flavored
     sugar-free gelatin
¾ cup boiling water
¾ cup cold water

1 tablespoon lemon juice
1 (8-ounce) container frozen fat-free
     whipped topping, thawed
2 cups chopped strawberries
Strawberry slices (optional)

Bake 1 (9-inch) piecrust according to package directions. Set aside.

Prepare gelatin according to package directions, using ¾ cup boiling water, ¾ cup cold water, and 1 tablespoon lemon juice. Chill 10 minutes or until consistency of unbeaten egg white.

Stir in whipped topping and chopped strawberries. Spoon into piecrust, mounding if necessary. Chill 3 hours or until set. Garnish with strawberry slices, if desired. **Yield:** 8 servings (serving size: 1 slice).

Per Serving: Calories 181   Fat 7.0g   (sat 3.0g)   Protein 1.8g   Carbohydrate 25.4g
Fiber 0.9g   Cholesterol 5mg   Sodium 138mg
Exchanges: 1 Starch, 1 Fruit, 1 Fat

4TH OF JULY BARBECUE

Serves 8

Chuck Roast Barbecue Sandwiches (page 200)

Corn-on-the-Cob (page 200)

Tangy Slaw (page 201)

Sliced tomatoes

Watermelon

Mint Chocolate Chip Ice Cream (page 201)

Chuck Roast Barbecue Sandwiches

Chuck Roast Barbecue Sandwiches

Prep: 10 minutes
Slow Cook: 6 to 9 hours

1 (2½-pound) boneless chuck roast, trimmed
2 onions, chopped
1 (12-ounce) can sugar-free cola-flavored beverage (1½ cups)
¼ cup Worcestershire sauce
1½ tablespoons apple cider vinegar or white vinegar
1 teaspoon beef bouillon granules
¾ teaspoon dry mustard
¾ teaspoon chili powder
¼ to ½ teaspoon ground red pepper
3 garlic cloves, minced
1 cup ketchup
1 tablespoon light butter
12 reduced-calorie hamburger buns

Place roast in a 3½- or 4-quart electric slow cooker; add onion. Combine cola and next 7 ingredients; cover and chill 1 cup sauce. Pour remaining sauce over roast. Cover with lid; cook on high-heat setting for 1 hour. Reduce heat setting to low; cook 8 hours or until roast is very tender. Remove roast with chopped onion from cooker, using a slotted spoon, and shred meat with 2 forks.

Combine reserved sauce, ketchup, and butter in a saucepan; cook over medium heat, stirring constantly, until thoroughly heated. Pour sauce over shredded meat, stirring gently. Spoon meat mixture onto buns. **Yield:** 12 servings (serving size: about 2 ounces cooked meat and 1 bun).

Per Serving: Calories 319 Fat 13.6g (sat 5.2g) Protein 23.7g Carbohydrate 27.6g
Fiber 3.5g Cholesterol 67mg Sodium 601mg
Exchanges: 2 Starch, 3 Lean Meat

Corn-on-the-Cob

Prep: 1 minute   Cook: 8 minutes

8 (6-inch) ears frozen corn
8 teaspoons yogurt-based spread
1 teaspoon salt
1 teaspoon pepper

Cook corn according to package directions. Spread yogurt spread over warm corn, and sprinkle with salt and pepper. **Yield:** 8 servings (serving size: 1 ear).

Per Serving: Calories 73 Fat 2.2g (sat 0.0g) Protein 1.9g Carbohydrate 14.0g
Fiber 1.6g Cholesterol 0mg Sodium 326mg
Exchange: 1 Starch

Tangy Slaw

Prep: 3 minutes

½ cup creamy mustard blend (such as
  Dijonnaise)
⅓ cup "measures-like-sugar" calorie-free
  sweetener

¼ cup cider vinegar
2 tablespoons apple cider
¼ cup sweet pickle relish
2 (7-ounce) packages shredded cabbage

Combine first 4 ingredients; stir well with a whisk. Combine pickle relish and cabbage in a bowl; pour dressing over slaw, and toss gently. Cover and chill. **Yield:** 8 (½-cup) servings.

Per Serving: Calories 48   Fat 1.5g   (sat 0.1g)   Protein 1.8g   Carbohydrate 8.9g
Fiber 1.4g   Cholesterol 0mg   Sodium 450mg
Exchanges: 2 Vegetable

Mint Chocolate Chip Ice Cream

Prep: 5 minutes

⅔ cup "measures-like-sugar" calorie-free
  sweetener
2 cups fat-free evaporated milk
1 cup fat-free milk
½ cup egg substitute

½ teaspoon imitation peppermint extract
6 drops green liquid food coloring
  (optional)
4 ounces bittersweet chocolate, coarsely
  chopped

Combine first 6 ingredients in a large bowl; beat with a mixer at medium speed until well blended. Stir in chocolate.
Pour mixture into freezer can of a 2-quart hand-turned or electric freezer. Freeze according to manufacturer's instructions. **Yield:** 12 (½-cup) servings.

Per Serving: Calories 97   Fat 2.9g   (sat 2.0g)   Protein 5.3g   Carbohydrate 12.7g
Fiber 0.0g   Cholesterol 2mg   Sodium 76mg
Exchange: 1 Skim Milk

Recipe Index

Nutrition Notes

Down Home Diabetic Recipes gives you the nutrition facts you want to know. We provide the following information with every recipe.

values are for one serving of the recipe

Per Serving:

Calories 299

Fat 2.0g (sat 0.4g)

Protein 22.8g

Carbohydrate 29.1g

total carbohydrate in one serving

grams are abbreviated "g"

Fiber 2.0 g

Cholesterol 47 mg

milligrams are abbreviated "mg"

Sodium 644mg

Exchanges 2 Starch, 2 Medium-Fat Meat

exchange values are for one serving

Nutritional Analyses

The nutritional values used in our calculations either come from a nutrient analysis computer program or are provided by food manufacturers. The values are based on the following assumptions:

- When we give a range for an ingredient, we calculate using the lesser amount.

- Only the amount of marinade absorbed is calculated.

- Garnishes and optional ingredients are not included in the analysis.

Diabetic Exchanges

Exchange values for all recipes are provided for people who use them for meal planning. The exchange values in this book are based on the *Exchange Lists for Meal Planning* developed by the American Diabetes Association and The American Dietetic Association.

Carbohydrate

If you count carbohydrate, look for the value in the nutrient analysis. The new American Diabetes Association guidelines loosen the restriction on sugar and encourage you to look at the total grams of carbohydrate in a serving. We have used small amounts of sugar in some recipes. We have also used a variety of sugar substitutes when the use of a substitute yields a quality product (see the Sugar Substitute Guide on page 20).

Sodium

Current dietary recommendations advise a daily sodium intake of 2,400 milligrams. We have limited the sodium in these recipes by using reduced-sodium products whenever possible.

If you must restrict sodium in your diet, please note the sodium value per serving and see if you should further modify the recipe.

The recipes that appear in this cookbook use the standard United States method for measuring liquid and dry or solid ingredients (teaspoons, tablespoons, and cups). The information in the following charts is provided to help cooks outside the U.S. successfully use these recipes. All equivalents are approximate.

EQUIVALENTS FOR DIFFERENT TYPES OF INGREDIENTS

A standard cup measure of a dry or solid ingredient will vary in weight depending on the type of ingredient. A standard cup of liquid is the same volume for any type of liquid. Use the following chart when converting standard cup measures to grams (weight) or milliliters (volume).

Standard Cup	Fine Powder (ex. flour)	Grain (ex. rice)	Granular (ex. sugar)	Liquid Solids (ex. butter)	Liquid (ex. milk)
1	140 g	150 g	190 g	200 g	240 ml
¾	105 g	113 g	143 g	150 g	180 ml
⅔	93 g	100 g	125 g	133 g	160 ml
½	70 g	75 g	95 g	100 g	120 ml
⅓	47 g	50 g	63 g	67 g	80 ml
¼	35 g	38 g	48 g	50 g	60 ml
⅛	18 g	19 g	24 g	25 g	30 ml

DRY INGREDIENTS BY WEIGHT

(To convert ounces to grams, multiply the number of ounces by 30.)

1 oz	=	¹⁄₁₆ lb	=	30 g
4 oz	=	¼ lb	=	120 g
8 oz	=	½ lb	=	240 g
12 oz	=	¾ lb	=	360 g
16 oz	=	1 lb	=	480 g

LENGTH

(To convert inches to centimeters, multiply the number of inches by 2.5.)

1 in	=					2.5 cm	
6 in	=	½ ft		=	15 cm		
12 in	=	1 ft		=	30 cm		
36 in	=	3 ft	=	1 yd	=	90 cm	
40 in	=				100 cm	=	1 m

LIQUID INGREDIENTS BY VOLUME

¼ tsp							1 ml		
½ tsp							2 ml		
1 tsp							5 ml		
3 tsp	=	1 tbls			=	½ fl oz	=	15 ml	
		2 tbls	=	⅛ cup	=	1 fl oz	=	30 ml	
		4 tbls	=	¼ cup	=	2 fl oz	=	60 ml	
		5⅓ tbls	=	⅓ cup	=	3 fl oz	=	80 ml	
		8 tbls	=	½ cup	=	4 fl oz	=	120 ml	
		10⅔ tbls	=	⅔ cup	=	5 fl oz	=	160 ml	
		12 tbls	=	¾ cup	=	6 fl oz	=	180 ml	
		16 tbls	=	1 cup	=	8 fl oz	=	240 ml	
		1 pt	=	2 cups	=	16 fl oz	=	480 ml	
		1 qt	=	4 cups	=	32 fl oz	=	960 ml	
						33 fl oz	=	1000 ml	= 1 liter

COOKING/OVEN TEMPERATURES

	Fahrenheit	Celsius	Gas Mark
Freeze Water	32° F	0° C	
Room Temperature	68° F	20° C	
Boil Water	212° F	100° C	
Bake	325° F	160° C	3
	350° F	180° C	4
	375° F	190° C	5
	400° F	200° C	6
	425° F	220° C	7
	450° F	230° C	8
Broil			Grill